The Witching Pool

JOHN PILKINGTON

CONTENTS

THE WITCHING POOL

ONE

In the spring of 1617, following that tempestuous Year of Astonishment, I reached my sixty-second birthday. Henceforth, after a hard winter - though tempered by a pleasant Christmas when Hester and I were joined by my daughter Anne and my beloved grandchild Kate - I was resolved to spend an untaxing year enjoying life on my modest acres. Fishing the Severn, of course, reading and sometimes riding to visit friends for cards and discourse. Life at Thirldon was pleasant enough, I decided, a far cry from the stench and corruption of London that had so disarmed me the year before.

The King, I heard, was now in Scotland, his first journey to his homeland since his coronation fourteen years earlier. Here in balmy Worcestershire all was quiet - until once again, by quirk of fate, an incident occurred which would throw my life into disarray. I wonder at times whether former magistrate Robert Belstrang is destined for a peaceful decline into slippered dotage, but must forever be leaving his fireside to undertake some further quest. But that Maytime I found myself caught up in a fearful business, that I feel it my duty to record. I speak of a dark cloud that passed over our corner of the county, whereby my peace of mind – let alone that of many others - was shaken to the core.

It began with the tragic death of a young maiden who was found drowned, only four miles south of Thirldon.

The news came to me on a visit into Worcester, where I had ridden to see my merchant about a consignment of French wines. I took dinner with my old friend Doctor Boyd, that dry and phlegmatic Scots physician whose company I had always enjoyed. We were leaving the Old Talbot Inn by the Minster, intending to take a stroll along the river before I collected Leucippus from the stables. Whereupon the good doctor, who had been silent for some minutes, mentioned that he intended to attend an inquest the following morning: that of a drowned girl, the eldest daughter of a landowner I knew Boyd heartily disliked, Giles Cobbett.

'But that's dreadful,' I exclaimed. 'When did it happen?'

'Two days ago, I believe. It seems a man whose dog had

strayed found the body. It's said that the girl took her own life. Susanna Cobbett – she was but seventeen years old.'

As I took in the grim tidings he added: 'A matter of the heart, perhaps. My own daughter was given to such extremes of feeling at that age, before she saw sense and married.'

'Well, I barely know the family,' I said. 'And from what I do know of Giles Cobbett, he's a cold-hearted man. Even so, such an event would be hard for any father to bear. Yet knowing your opinion of him, I wonder at your interest.'

'The act of self-murder has always been of interest to me,' my friend answered. 'What drives people to such desperation – or wickedness, as some would term it? In truth I've never had much sympathy for those who stoop to it, but I'm curious to hear the evidence.'

I asked him where the proceedings were being held.

'In a tithe barn at Powick,' came the reply. 'It's close to where the crime was committed – that is, a pond on the edge of Newland wood, a mile or so south of the village.'

I stopped. 'Good God, do you mean the Witching Pool?'

'The very place. But I've no more patience with such superstitious chaff than you have.'

'Well, this will set tongues wagging,' I said. 'The pool's reputation goes back a long way.'

'It may well do,' Boyd said. 'Though I never heard of anyone drowning themselves there.'

As we began to stroll again, I pictured the tree-shrouded pond from memory: a gloomy place. 'As I recall, it's shallow enough to stand up in,' I said. 'Of little use to a sporting man - unless you're fishing for minnows.'

'That's another reason the case interests me. The girl must have been most determined, to see the business through.'

He wore an expression I knew well: Boyd had long been a sceptic, and hence a man after my own heart. After pondering the matter, I slowed my pace. 'I should be getting home. Hester has been at the Thirldon account books. She likes me to look them over, not that I can ever improve on her handiwork.'

Boyd nodded, and we turned about to retrace our steps. 'If the verdict tomorrow is that the Cobbett girl took her own life, it will pose difficulties for her father,' he observed.

'Because a suicide may not be buried in consecrated ground?'

'Indeed. And as I've said, I'm curious to hear the circumstances.'

'Well, you've aroused my curiosity too,' I told him. 'I'm almost tempted to ride down to Powick with you tomorrow. Do you know who will hold the inquest?'

'I believe Justice Standish will preside,' Boyd answered, with a sidelong glance at me. 'He's not merely magistrate, he's acting coroner at present.' When my face fell, he suppressed a smile. 'No friend of yours, as I recall.'

I made no reply. It was no secret that Matthew Standish and I disliked each other. Back in 1612, when I was obliged to step down as magistrate, the man had pretended sympathy at my downfall. Yet I had never trusted him: a sour-faced pedant. To be in his company was the last thing I desired.

'Hence, I'll understand if you prefer not to ride to Powick with me in the morning,' my friend murmured.

'Now I think upon it, I meant to speak to my gardeners tomorrow about the fruit trees,' I said.

Boyd nodded sagely.

***

It was a warm afternoon, and I rode Leucippus at a leisurely pace back to Thirldon. The blossom had flown now, and the trees were in full leaf. In truth, the topic of Susanna Cobbett's sad death had all but slipped my mind by the time I entered the courtyard. As I dismounted on the cobbles my groom Elkins appeared, wearing what I termed his 'important' face: news awaited me.

'I trust you passed a pleasant time in town, sir,' he began. And as I handed him the reins: 'There's a fellow waiting to see you. Been here all day, he has.'

'Someone we know?' I enquired.

He shook his head. 'He's from downriver, towards Clevelode. Cottager, I believe.'

'Have you an inkling what it's about?'

'I haven't, sir,' Elkins answered. He placed a hand on Leucippus's neck, ruffling his mane; they were old friends. 'But he had a face as long as a pikestaff.'

I sighed, and left him to his work. It was not unknown for people to seek me out for advice, though they knew I'd long since quitted the magistrate's bench. I seldom saw payment beyond a clutch of eggs, perhaps, or a gamebird at Christmas. Given the poverty of most smallholders, I expected nothing from my visitor. But I was curious. And when I got myself inside the house, to be greeted by Hester, I grew alert.

'The visitor's name is Edward Mason. He walked all the way from Newland. It's a grave matter – he's a frightened man.'

'Did he say what it's about?'

'Very little. You'd better let him explain.'

I turned to walk towards my private parlour, whereupon she stayed me. 'He waits in the kitchen. We gave him a bit of dinner, for which he was most grateful.'

Without further word I went to the rear of the house and entered Thirldon's kitchen. The wenches bobbed and proceeded to look busy, while Henry, my cook, greeted me briefly before jerking a thumb towards the corner of the room. As I turned, a shambling figure in rough countryman's garb jumped up from a stool and made a clumsy bow. He stood awkwardly as I came forward, meaning to put him at ease.

'You are Edward Mason?'

'I am, Master Justice. I'd be most obliged if you would… that is, I need to know what to do, and… well…'

He broke off, tongue-tied as could be. Did I truly strike such a forbidding attitude nowadays, I wondered? I offered my hand, which he shook vigorously.

'I hear you've waited most of the day,' I said. 'Your pardon for that. It's pleasant outdoors - shall we walk together?'

The man's look of relief was answer enough. And no sooner had he and I ventured out into the kitchen garden than he began to speak, his words tumbling over themselves in haste.

'It's my mother, Master Justice - Agnes Mason. Lives with me and my family on our bit of land, over Newland way. She's a healer… folk come to her for salves and such. You might have heard of her – Mother Agnes?'

The name may have struck a distant bell, but I shook my head and bade him continue.

'The matter is, sir…' the man looked away. 'I'm almost afeared to speak of it, but I must.'

'Indeed, since it clearly troubles you,' I replied. 'Has something happened to your mother?'

'It has, sir…' he gave a sigh. 'She's been took, by the constables. There were three of 'em - as if she's the strength to resist any man, being in her sixtieth year. But it was so ordered – and now she's imprisoned, in Worcester!'

'On what charge?' I asked, with a frown coming on.

The man hesitated, then: 'They're calling her a witch.' And when my frown deepened, he added: 'In fact, 'tis worse than that, sir - she's accused of causing death by witchery. That's murder, is it not?'

He was most agitated - indeed, he was close to tears. For myself, I was silent. Our time is one of dread for some people – mainly women, and often elderly, like Agnes Mason – who find themselves accused of witchcraft. In almost every case, to my mind, the charge is false, but the outcome is seldom in doubt: severe punishment for a first conviction, then death by hanging for a second. In some countries, they burn the poor creatures alive.

'Causing death…?' On a sudden a thought struck me, as my conversation with Dr Boyd came flooding back. 'Whose death is she accused of bringing about?' I demanded, somewhat sharply.

Mason swallowed, then made his answer - but even before the words were out, I knew.

'One by the name of Susanna, sir… a well-bred maid, the daughter of Giles Cobbett of Ebbfield. She's gone and drowned herself in the old pool on the border of our land – and they're saying she was bewitched by my mother, and driven to madness. Now, we fear Agnes will face the gallows!'

He stared at me. 'In God's name, Master Justice: Cobbett is our landlord, and a gentleman. What am I to do?'

TWO

I clearly recall that conversation with Edward Mason, as he and I walked about the garden in the waning sunlight. After he had told his tale he appeared spent, hanging his head in mingled fear and anguish. The matter was stark: the very day after his daughter's death, Giles Cobbett himself had brought a charge of murder by witchcraft against his own tenant, Mason's ageing mother, claiming he had evidence of conjuration. Agnes had been taken not to the prison in Worcester but to the Guildhall, where the cellars were sometimes used for confinement. There she was to await trial at the next Assizes, which would be at Midsummer. This much her son learned from the sergeant-at-arms, a man called John Lisle whom I knew. Lisle was an officer of good character, and would have carried out his orders with efficiency, though I doubt he relished the task.

'See now, the evening draws near,' I said at last. 'Will you stay to eat supper? Then I'll take you back to your farm, if you care to ride double on my horse. He's a strong beast.'

'With all my heart, sir,' Mason answered. 'And I offer you my thanks-'

'Well, I've done nothing to earn them,' I told him. 'I've yet to decide what course of action to take. But I'd like to pause on our ride and reacquaint myself with that infamous pond, if you're willing. There should be enough daylight left, if we don't tarry long.'

At that the man gave a start. 'The Witching Pool? Why would you wish to see it?'

'Call it curiosity,' I replied.

'But, Master Justice...' he grew agitated again. 'It's not a wholesome place... we never go near it. And with what's happened-'

'What, do you think the ghost of Susanna Cobbett haunts it?' I asked. But seeing his expression, I relented. 'See now, there's nothing to fear. I would merely like to look upon the scene of the alleged crime. If I'm to assist your mother, I need to gather as much intelligence as I can. Do you see?'

Mason blinked. 'Then, you will aid us?'

'Let's go to supper,' I said.

***

It was a ride of about five miles to Mason's smallholding, a journey we undertook in silence. In the still evening, with my passenger pressed against my back, I rode Leucippus southwards towards the River Teme, crossing it via the old bridge at Powick. Here, I recalled, the inquest into the Cobbett girl's death was to take place on the morrow. And now, I found myself revising my decision not to attend with Boyd. In the light of what I had learned, it could be worthwhile after all.

The village was quiet as we passed through, following the west bank of the Severn before turning on to a track which led to Newland Wood. We were now on the border of Giles Cobbett's land, which lay on both sides of the river. His own manor of Ebbfield was on the far side, but could be reached by a ferry. On this side was the small farm of one of his tenants, a man named Abel Humphreys. Bordering Humphreys' farm on the west was the tiny smallholding of the Mason family, which we now approached. After proceeding another hundred paces, with the trees to our right, I reined in.

'I seem to recall that the pool is just through there,' I said, turning in the saddle to point. 'Is it not?'

Somewhat glumly, Mason nodded. 'There's a path just ahead, though it's seldom used.'

'Let's dismount,' I told him, being in some discomfort.

We did so. And leaving Leucippus to await my return, I allowed the other to lead the way through the long grass until we were among the trees. The ancient wood, rich in oaks and beeches, soon closed about us, the air alive with birdsong. After a short time, the ground dipped and the pool appeared – dark with weed and, I have to admit, somewhat forbidding. It was no more than thirty or forty paces across, overhung with alders and willows. Pond skaters skittered across the surface, but otherwise the water was like glass. Curiously enough, the birds had ceased to sing by the time I walked to its edge. Mason hung back, his unease plain to see.

'Do you know if anyone has searched hereabouts?' I asked him.

'Searched for what, Master Justice?'

'For anything untoward. Signs of a struggle, a scrap of clothing, or…?'

He was shaking his head. 'I know nothing of that, sir-' on a sudden he stiffened, his eyes on a tree behind me. Turning sharply, I found myself looking at a dead bird hanging from a branch - I should say *tied* to a branch by its feet, head downwards. It was a crow, a common enough sight – but what was uncommon was the plaited cord about its neck. Woven into the cord was what looked like a lock of hair. I took a step forward to observe the object more closely, when a cry from Mason made me stop.

'Don't, Master, I beg you. It's a thing of evil - a token.'

'Do you truly think so?' In full sceptic humour, I turned to face him. 'Then what, pray, do you think it signifies?'

'I know not, sir… a warning, perhaps.'

He lowered his gaze. Worcestershire folk are of course well-known for their old superstitions, my own servant Childers included. I sighed and was about to make some further remark, whereupon Mason raised his arm and pointed, this time to a spot further off.

'See, there's more!'

I followed his gaze and saw another dead bird – a thrush - bound to a twig, with something about its neck.

'Well, this is most curious,' I said. 'It's almost as if someone placed these tokens, as you term them, to frighten people away. Is it not?'

The man met my eye. 'Well sir, I've seen things myself… when I was younger, and came a-fishing here with a friend.'

'Fishing, you say? Did you catch anything?' I enquired, meaning to divert him from these gloomy thoughts. His answer, however, caused me to frown.

'Nothing we could eat. A great newt, which took my worm most greedily. But it was what came after that frighted me – frighted us both.' He paused, discomforted by the memory, until I urged him to say more.

'Something moved in the pool… something so big it made the water swell, dashing a small wave upon the bank.' He drew a breath. 'There's no creature large enough to do that, sir - not in a pond like this.'

'Did you try to see what it was?' I asked. 'The water's not deep - a man could wade across.'

'Do you jest, Master Justice?' Mason shook his head quickly. 'We did no such thing, but turned tail and ran! This is a grim place – do you not feel it? Why, it's been said…' He broke off, which naturally aroused my interest further.

'What's been said, Master Edward?' I enquired. 'Come, I've given you hospitality and brought you home. Will you not return the favour by satisfying an old man's curiosity?'

He hesitated, then: 'I'm loth to speak of it, sir – I mean, after what's happened. But some say this was a place where witches held their Sabbaths - midnight revels, with their familiars and such.' The man almost shuddered. 'Can we not leave now? It will grow dark soon, and my wife will wonder what's become of me.'

His unease was such, I could only indicate my assent. I recalled now that I might have had heard such tales myself - and hence I could not resist posing a question which occurred.

'Your mother, Agnes… did she ever come here?'

At that, the other was aghast. 'In God's name, Master Justice, do you too believe she's a witch?' He cried. 'That she could do the wickedness she's accused of – you of all people? If that's so, why do you-'

But when I held up a hand, he stopped himself.

'I'm very much in doubt of it,' I said. 'But you must expect such questions to be asked of your mother, when she comes to trial. I merely wish to gather facts.'

I sighed, and could not help experiencing a shiver; then, the air was growing cool. 'But I agree that we've tarried here long enough,' I continued. 'Shall we retrace our steps?'

Mason showed his relief and turned away – whereupon a noise from somewhere across the pool made us both stop in our tracks. It was a rustling, as of branches being disturbed. I swung round, peering into the trees, but could see nothing – until a sound rang out that startled even me.

It was laughter: a short, barking laugh, eerie enough yet unmistakably human. Swiftly I looked round at Mason, expecting him to be terrified – but instead, the man had relaxed.

'That's Berritt,' he said. And when I raised my brows: 'Old Ned Berritt… been a part of these woods since I was a boy. Does a bit of rat-catching, fishes for eels in the river, and not averse to poaching. Likely he's been watching us, ever since we got here.'

He gestured towards the path. 'Now will you come to my house sir, and take a mug of ale before you ride home?'

***

A short while later I was seated by the fire in Mason's small cottage nursing a mug of farm-brewed ale, somewhat embarrassed by the reproach the man was receiving from his young wife. Isabel Mason was small and plump, her face somewhat ruddy, its hue heightened by indignation. To that she had already given some vent, standing over her husband who sat in an old oaken settle opposite me.

'You said you'd walk into Worcester, see Mother Agnes and get yourself home soon after noon,' Mistress Mason chided. 'Yet now I hear you never even saw her - so how do we know what condition she's in? Instead you went a-bothering Master Belstrang, to no purpose I can see…' She stopped herself, took a breath and faced me.

'I ask pardon, Master Justice, for I mean no slight to you. I've heard how you've been kind to folk, like you've been good to Edward today. Only the matter is…' She glanced at her husband. 'The matter is, sir, I've been at my wit's end since Agnes was taken, and that's the plain truth. Scarce an hour goes by when I don't expect more bad news – even that we could lose our home! He knows it as well as I do.'

She indicated Edward, who sat so dejectedly, had matters been different I might have felt inclined to laugh. But this family's case being so grave, I chose the moment to speak.

'I know that Giles Cobbett is your landlord, Mistress,' I said. 'But do you not hold a secure lease on this land? I speak now as a man of the law. If the lease is for a fixed term then it would be difficult for him to evict you for any reason, so long as the rent is paid. On the other hand, if it's a *Tenancy at Will*, he has the right.'

I turned to Mason and asked him if he was the copyholder.

'My father held the lease, sir,' came the reply. 'On his death it passed to my mother, by his will. But if she's convicted for murder, I fear Sir Giles will have grounds… might it be so?'

I pondered the matter. 'If there's anything in the lease a lawyer might seize upon, then I suppose it might,' I allowed, which caused both of them to draw breath. And though I had no wish to alarm them further, I thought it best to continue.

'In truth, However, there are other factors you should consider,' I told them. 'For one, in the sad event that Agnes is convicted, I believe it would be most difficult for you to remain here. People's feelings would be so hardened against you, I hesitate to think what might occur-'

'You mean folk would come at us?' Mistress Mason broke in. 'With pitchforks and torches? God in heaven, Master, tell us it isn't so! I've two children asleep up in the loft, and moreover-'

She stopped herself again - and in a moment I understood. I looked at Mason and found his eyes upon me.

'Moreover, there's another child coming, sir, is what she would have said,' he muttered. 'Now you see our condition.'

I gave a nod. Mistress Mason, for her part, said nothing further, but sat down heavily beside her husband. But if she was moved to tears, she would not allow them. She was a spirited young woman, who had won not only my sympathies but my respect too.

And all at once I knew my course was clear, as I believe I had known since I spoke with Edward Mason that afternoon. As I now knew that I would not be riding to Powick in the morning with Doctor Boyd, to attend the inquest of Susanna Cobbett.

'If I might venture an opinion, Mistress,' I said, 'your husband did right in coming to me, instead of going to the Guildhall. There's little he could have done for his mother; he might even have been refused leave to see her. You are in a dangerous place, and what paths exist – if indeed there are such – are hidden from you. The Justice who will try Agnes at the Assizes is unknown to me; he may be of the sort who will take against her on sight. But if you're willing, I will visit her in the morning and see how the land lies. Thereafter, if I believe there is a chance of acquittal, I will try to carry the business forward. Though I must forbear to raise your hopes. This is a delicate matter, for which-'

But my speech was stilled, for at once Isabel Mason got up and bent to clasp my free hand in both of hers. With such precipitation, I might add, that I was hard pressed to avoid spilling the contents of my mug over my knees.

'May the Lord bless you, Master Belstrang,' she burst out. 'For I expected help from no-one – let alone one who once sat as a magistrate! You've brought us hope – precious hope, in our darkest hour…' She looked away. 'But we cannot pay you, sir. It pains me to say it, but…'

'Isabel!'

Edward Mason spoke sharply. At last finding his voice, along with some of his self-worth, the man stood up, took his wife by the shoulders and eased her gently back to the settle. He was not angry: his concern had to do with her condition. As she sat down again, he gathered himself and turned to me.

'Our blessings on you, Master Justice,' he said. 'Along with our heartfelt thanks, no matter what befalls us. Howsoever you advise us, it shall be done – this I swear.'

'Well, you must know that I cannot make any promises,' I replied. I was moved not only by the couple's plight but by their faith in my powers, which I knew were somewhat slight. 'But I will poke about, as folk say I do, and, well…'

With an attempt at a smile I trailed off, drained my mug and rose to my feet. 'I can only urge you not to lose hope,' I ended, only too aware of how lame the words sounded.

Thereafter I took my leave of them as dusk was falling, and was soon urging Leucippus to a canter, back towards Powick and thence home.

An urge was upon me to help this family if I could. Yet quite soon a gloom stole over me, when I thought on the promise I had made for the morrow. Somehow, I had taken it upon myself to visit a woman accused of murder by witchcraft – one who, in the eyes of just about everyone from the Mayor down to the lowliest beggar, was in all likelihood already adjudged guilty.

This was a cloud, I realised, that would take some effort to shift.

THREE

The next morning was breezy, and somewhat advanced before I at last rode over the bridge and entered the city by the West Gate. For in truth, I had little appetite for the task ahead.

Worcester was a-bustle, with people of every rank going their ways, a few of them recognising me as I walked Leucippus through the streets. Doing my best to seem of good cheer, I returned their salutations before dismounting and finding a horse-holder. I then made my way to the Guildhall on foot and spoke briefly to the porter. Once inside, I sought out Sergeant Lisle. By good fortune he was found, and after an exchange of greetings, away from the eyes and ears of clerks and others who passed by, I came to the matter in hand.

'Agnes Mason?' The tall sergeant, solid and heavy-bearded, never seemed to change with the passage of years. Eying me shrewdly, he raised an eyebrow. 'Might I ask what brings you to see her, Master Justice?' Lisle was another of those who used my former title as a mark of respect, which was not displeasing to me, coming from him.

'I'm acquainted with the family,' I said. 'They're much dismayed. I understand it was you who arrested the woman?'

'I did. I was told to take men with me and expect resistance, but there was none. She came as meek as a lamb.'

'Well now, what do you make of the business?' I ventured. There was no need to waste words with Lisle, though he appeared to dislike the question.

'I don't quite take your meaning, sir.'

'What I mean, sergeant, is do you believe she's a witch?' I returned. 'That she would cause a young girl to lose her senses and drown herself? For I'll admit I find it unlikely. What could she possibly gain by such a deed?'

'Master Justice…' the other gave a sigh and shook his head. 'You know better than to ask such things of me. I'm not paid to have opinions, only to do my office.'

'I ask not as a former Justice, but as a friend, if I might call you so,' I told him. 'We've known each other a long time, have we not? As I know you're not a man to rush to judgement.'

He hesitated, then looked aside briefly. 'There are rumours aplenty,' he murmured. 'But I'll not deny that the woman seems harmless enough to me. That's as far as I'll go.'

I was curious now. 'What kind of rumours would those be?' I asked. But at that, a look came over the man's face which I remembered well: one of plain obstinacy.

'I've said that's as far as I'll go, sir,' he answered. 'Now, since you seem determined to see the prisoner, I'll conduct you to the cellars.'

He waited, whereupon I allowed him to lead the way. Down the stairs we walked, Lisle ahead with keys jangling at his belt. The floor below was gloomy, stone-flagged and lit by torches. There were few prisoners here, most being confined in the old chamber at the ruined castle. Hence the newest arrival had been given a room to herself, at the end of the passage where we stopped. Lisle fitted the key, opened the door and stood aside, allowing me to enter the tiny cell.

It was so dark that I could see little, but at last I made out a pallet of straw and a pail in the corner. The place looked empty, until a slender figure materialised from the gloom. I stopped abruptly, whereupon the prisoner spoke – not in the cracked voice of an old crone, which I confess I had expected, but in one as soft and mellow as any I have heard.

'You wish to see me, sir? Then you're most welcome – how can I aid you?'

***

We stood, she and I, for in the absence of even a stool we could do no other. Having assured Lisle I would call him if I were in need, the sergeant closed the door upon us. He would not lock it, he said, but a watch would be kept, though to my mind such action was needless. For my immediate impression of this woman was not only that she presented no danger to anyone, but rather the opposite. She was a healer, her son had said, the day before at Thirldon. She had thought I was come to ask advice about some remedy as, it emerged, one person who knew her had already done. Hence her surprise was great when

15

she learned the reason for my visit, and almost at once she was asking after her family.

'Edward's a good man and a good father,' Agnes Mason told me, after I had given her what reassurance I could. She stood erect and composed in her plain frock and apron, her hair long and unbound. 'But he's not much of a farmer. You'll have seen they're poor folk, sir. If the worst happens, they won't be able to put up a fight against Giles Cobbett. Mayhap you don't know him, but he's a man who'll have his way.'

'I know him a little,' I said.

'For years he's wanted our piece of land, for sowing he claims,' she went on. 'To add to Humphreys' acres, so he can raise the rent – I speak of my neighbour, Abel Humphreys. Though both of them know the land's good for little but pasture. We keep pigs, a cow and a few hens…' she sighed. 'But you won't want to hear me complain, sir. I'm thankful, and sore amazed that you've come here. What shall I tell you? Ask what you will.'

I was silent for a while, marshalling my thoughts. In truth, before meeting Agnes Mason I had been inclined to adopt my magistrate's manner, and put her to question as I would have done anyone suspected of wrongdoing. But now I was in a quandary, for her very presence had dashed aside any prejudices I harboured. So: I will confess it now, and have done with it.

Agnes was but a little short of sixty years old, her hair silvered with age. Yet she had the face, manner and shape of a woman of fifteen or even twenty years younger – and to my great surprise, I was sorely attracted to her.

There, I have said it. And the mixture of feelings that arose, as she and I talked, threatened to become a trial in my mind. I thought briefly of my dead wife, and of Hester; I had barely looked at anyone of the other sex in ten years, and was content - or so I told myself. Yet here, in an odorous and gloomy cell, accused of a heinous crime, was a woman with cornflower-blue eyes that looked steadily into mine as she spoke, and disarmed me utterly.

It was almost as if Robert Belstrang were bewitched.

'Ask what I will, you say…' I gave a cough, shook myself

16

inwardly and tried to behave like the lawyer I had been. 'Well, perhaps you should give me your version of events, any way you please. Touching especially, perhaps, on your feelings towards your landlord.'

'There's little to tell,' Agnes said, after a pause. 'I was taken by the sergeant, with nothing said beyond the charges, and brought here. As for feelings, I have few of any sort towards Cobbett. I rarely see him, and I see less of his daughters. He keeps them on a tight leash at Ebbfield, even the eldest… or so he did.'

She lowered her gaze. 'That poor maid, as pretty as they come. To take her own life – it's a most hellish thing, which has caused me troubling thoughts.' She looked up, then: 'But one thing I swear, Master Belstrang: I'd no more have wished harm on that girl than I would on my own grandchildren.'

Her voice rose as she delivered the last words, and by instinct I regarded her keenly. At such times, in the past, I always tried to read a suspect's gaze, seeking any trace of deception. But there was none; I felt certain of it, and my heart turned at the injustice that was being meted out to this woman. I must have given myself away, for in the next moment a slight smile appeared.

'You believe me,' Agnes said quietly.

'Well now, let's suppose for the moment that I do,' I replied. 'Even so, your case is most difficult, Mistress… some might say hopeless.' I drew a breath. 'Perhaps you could venture an explanation as to why Cobbett has taken the terrible step that he has? To accuse you of bewitching his daughter to such a fearful extent that she became mad - mad enough to travel some distance from her home, and drown herself in a stagnant pond?'

To that Agnes made no answer. Her smile faded, but she continued to look steadily at me.

'Come now,' I urged. 'You must know that a man like Cobbett would never do this unless he believes he has a case? Whatever else he is, he's no fool. He'll have to give evidence at trial, for one thing-'

'You are mistaken, sir,' Agnes interrupted. 'He is a fool, in some ways – a rich man, but a man like any other. For he too believed I had powers I do not possess, though I'm loth to speak of it.'

'But you must,' I exclaimed, frowning. 'Any scrap of evidence could be valuable, when you come to trial. You face the gallows. Whatever has passed between you and your landlord, you should…'

I fell silent then, feeling something of a fool myself. Any man of a certain age who looked upon Agnes might imagine what had passed. Cobbett was a widower, and there was his humble tenant, a handsome widow… I was about to try and put the notion into words, as delicately as I could, when she spoke up somewhat sharply.

'Oh no – not that.'

She looked displeased. 'He never came to me for the reason you're thinking,' she said, with a shake of her head. 'There are some who believe I have unearthly powers, merely because I'm the seventh child of a seventh child. Or because I retain good health for my years, and have some skills passed from my mother in herb-lore and such.' She drew breath. 'But I'm not a cunning-woman sir, and never was.'

'Well… in truth, Mistress, I incline to the same opinion,' I said with some relief. 'But see now, you must say more if I'm to help you. For I grow convinced that the charge Cobbett has brought is but a scheme. Perhaps, in his grief, he wishes to cast blame away from himself for his daughter's demise. Or more likely he wishes to take possession of your land - you've as good as said so yourself.'

I waited. For a moment she seemed to debate with herself, then: 'I'm loth to break my word, when anyone asks me to swear secrecy,' she said. 'But it was a fool's errand. I told him so, yet he wouldn't listen. I speak of the day he caught me alone on the road - more than a year back, it was. He wished me to use my skills, he said, to find gold.'

And when I merely stared at her: 'It's an old tale, at Madresfield and Clevelode and the country round about. Have you heard of Offa's Gold, sir?'

I shook my head.

'Folk used to say there's a trove buried somewhere near our

farm,' Agnes said. 'Saxon gold from the time of the Kings of Mercia, hidden after some battle when they were in flight. There's no truth to it, I'm certain. But Cobbett's a greedy man, there's few would deny it. He'd seen some old map, he said, and...' she shrugged. 'In short, he demanded I do my utmost by conjuration, to divine for Offa's Gold as some folk divine for water. He would pay me a share, he said, so that my family need never fret about rent again. Those were his words... but when I told him it was beyond me to attempt such a task, he grew angry. I believe that's the last time he and I spoke. Now Edward always goes to pay the rent...' Her face clouded. 'Isabel too dislikes Cobbett heartily. She's a daughter to me... I cannot bear to think on it now, with her carrying another child as she is.'

She was silent, having said all she wished; indeed, to my mind there was little more she needed to say. And yet, proving her testimony would be a task of Sisyphean magnitude. My heart sank at the thought.

For the plain fact was, Cobbett was a powerful man who, for some reason, had set himself against Agnes. He would have taken steps – and for one thing, I had little hope now that the inquest into his daughter's death would shed much light. I thought suddenly of Boyd, and resolved to see him as soon as he returned from Powick.

For the present I could only take my leave of Agnes, and as I had done with her family, urge her to retain what hopes she could. I would return, I promised, though I was uncertain when.

'You are kind,' was all she said. She watched as I stepped to the door, opened it and turned to bid her farewell; then she favoured me with a smile that touched my heart.

There was a guard in the passage outside, but it wasn't Sergeant Lisle. Instead I found myself facing a squat man with a bald pate, wearing a sneer. Having lost no time in slamming the cell door and locking it, he spat on the flagstones and eyed me.

'She didn't turn you into a toad, then?'

I blinked, and my gorge rose in an instant. 'Sir,' I snapped. 'You may not know me, fellow, but I was a Justice here. Kindly remember your place.'

'Oh... I beg your pardon – *sir,*' the fellow retorted. Still smirking, he made a half-bow. ''Twas your welfare I was concerned about, nothing more. You should have taken a phial of holy water in with you. It's not often we play host to witches – a man can't be too careful.'

With an effort, I held my tongue; it was a waste of breath to do otherwise. I turned to make my way back to the stairs, then paused. 'Your name?' I enquired.

'It's Burton, sir.' The smirk was still in place. 'I pray you, call upon me any time.'

'Perhaps I will, Master Burton,' I said. 'For I intend to come again. In the meantime, be sure that you deal fairly with your prisoner – I'll enquire of her how matters stand. And...' this with as hard a look as I could summon: 'That woman's no more a witch than you are. Though I'll not say which one of you reminds me of a toad – you may ponder it yourself.'

Whereupon I strode to the stairs and climbed to the ground floor, into the welcome light of day.

FOUR

That afternoon, having taken a light dinner, I called upon Doctor Boyd at his house in Sudbury Street, where I told him of the events of the day before and of my meeting with Agnes. But he was distracted, and I would soon learn the cause: the inquest at Powick, he announced, had been an utter sham.

'A comedy, Robert,' the good doctor growled. 'It was all over within two hours. I hardly know where to begin. Shall I tell you first, that no-one had even troubled to examine the deceased's body? Or that no attempt was made to establish how she got to the place where she died? Or that the man who found the body was not even called? Or should I remind you that Cobbett's seat at Ebbfield is a moated manor-house, in the old Tudor style? Yet no-one enquired as to why a maid bent on self-murder would trouble to cross the mighty Severn, venture into a wood and drown herself in a shallow pond, when she could have done the deed but yards from her own door. Can you believe it?'

'What about witnesses?' I enquired.

Boyd spread his hands. 'Such witnesses as were called were supporters of Cobbett, chief among them being his tenant Humphreys. A sly sort, in my opinion. He spoke of the deceased as being of frail disposition, hinting that she was likely of unsound mind too. While her poor, widowed father had struggled to bring his daughters up alone, at great sacrifice. To hear him speak you'd have thought Cobbett was a saint, instead of the grasping landowner we know him to be.' He sighed. 'I tell you, Robert, the whole business appeared as a paean to Cobbett in his loss, with scant attention paid to his dead daughter.'

'What of Standish?' I enquired. 'Did he not try to uncover the true events of that night, when the girl took her life?'

'Well now, that's the oddest part of it, to my mind,' Boyd answered. 'For reasons best known to himself, Justice Standish appeared eager to draw proceedings to a close as swiftly as possible. Whether from mere distaste, or a lack of evidence...'

he shrugged. 'But there was no doubt in the minds of the jury... poor villagers, mostly. The verdict, as you will have surmised, was suicide. And Cobbett emerged as a man most cruelly wronged, deserving the sympathy of all who were present. In fact, his own evidence caused a minor sensation...' he frowned. 'And doubtless it bodes ill for your new friend, Mistress Mason.'

'How so?' I asked, somewhat sharply.

'Let me say that, for those who enjoy a play, it was a good performance,' Boyd said. 'To summarize, he swore that the witch had cursed him, because he refused her charity in the late hard winter. He said Mason went upon her knees and cursed him thrice in a bold and wicked manner, telling him his firstborn would perish within the coming year. All of that, he claimed, done with signs and incantations he did not understand. As I said, his testimony was most engaging, and generated dismay among those present. Why would it not?'

I was silent then, eyes lowered as a gloom fell upon me. I knew that, in any court of law, such report from a man of Cobbett's status would be believed, while in the absence of any witness to the contrary, few if any would believe Agnes.

I looked up, and found Boyd's eyes upon me.

'The die is cast, Robert,' he said gravely. 'Whoever presides at the Assizes will dispense whatever justice he thinks expedient. But given the strong feelings against anyone accused of witchery, from the King himself down...' he shook his head. 'From an acquaintance of mine who was present, I gather that the Bishop himself is taking an interest in the case. John Thornborough detests witches, whether real or imagined. I fear Agnes Mason was adjudged guilty from the moment her arrest was ordered.' He paused. 'As for poor Susanna Cobbett-'

'As for Susanna Cobbett,' I broke in, 'being named a suicide, her burial will be a matter of contention.'

'Well, not quite,' Boyd said. 'The parson at Powick is unwilling to bury her, it seems, but that didn't appear to trouble Cobbett unduly. The funeral service will take place tomorrow in the chapel at Ebbfield, with the burial to follow close by. A convenient solution, would you not agree?'

I made no reply. Turning the matter about, I pictured Edward and Isabel Mason in their cottage, faces drawn with worry. Then I saw Agnes standing in her cell, calm and smiling. Had she compassed her coming death, I wondered, and accepted it?

Boyd spoke again, pulling me from my reverie. 'As a close friend, Robert,' he said, 'I'd advise you to step away from this business. Yet as a friend, I also know such counsel is probably fruitless. I see how the matter has affected you. And I will aid you if I can, but I suspect it is beyond us both. The inquest report will be used in the Mason woman's trial. Whatever transpires, I fear she's doomed to die.'

'And yet,' I said, as the notion sprang up, 'I have a mind to attend the funeral tomorrow.' And when my friend showed surprise: 'As another landowner, if not quite a neighbour, it would be but a matter of courtesy to pay my respects.'

The doctor said nothing; he was familiar enough with the Belstrang stubbornness.

'I've not seen Cobbett for some time,' I added. 'And though the circumstances are not of our choosing, I'm curious to see how the man conducts himself, in the light of his dreadful loss.'

'Well now…' Boyd peered at me from beneath his untidy eyebrows. 'I do believe you've taken up the accused's cause already.' And as another thought struck him: 'I've no desire to go myself, if that's the way your mind moves,' he said with a frown. 'I've said I will aid you, but-'

'Be at ease,' I replied. 'Call it a whim, call it what you will, but this is something I should undertake alone.'

My friend gave a sigh. 'Then again, I'll admit that your curiosity is contagious,' he said. 'I'd be interested to know of any movement… will you inform me?'

I nodded, and rose to take my leave.

But as to the matter of attending the funeral of Susanna Cobbett alone, on my return to Thirldon I would learn that Hester was of a different opinion.

***

Supper was a quiet affair that evening, as my preoccupation with events weighed upon me. My steward Childers, far from being his usual dour self, was at pains to lighten matters, speaking of the birth of a foal that was somewhat late, but had passed without difficulty. More, the fruit trees were in health, and those in the know predicted a bounteous harvest. He continued in this vein for some time before deducing that I was barely listening, and ceased his prattle. It fell to Hester to draw me into speech.

'You've been silent long enough, sir,' she murmured, taking a sip of malmsey. 'Would you care to tell us what kept you in Worcester all day?'

I nodded, and pushed aside my pudding; I had but small appetite. Sharing my news with those closest to me would perhaps help me review the matter, as it had often done in the past. So, after fortifying myself with a gulp of wine I gave my account, though I confess it was somewhat brief in regard to my meeting with Agnes. Having ended with my leave-taking of Boyd, I sat back and allowed my listeners to digest at leisure. Naturally enough, Childers was first to speak.

'God in heaven, sir, this is a tale most terrible,' he exclaimed, with a shake of his head.

'It is,' I agreed, with a glance at Hester.

'Witchery, but a few miles from where we sit?' His face clouded. 'I haven't heard the like in years.'

'I don't believe it's anything of the sort,' I said, somewhat curtly.

'So, what will you do?' He asked. And when I made no response: 'If you care to hear my opinion, it would be most troublesome to you, if you–'

'Indeed so,' I broke in. 'Doubtless you'll counsel me as Boyd did, to withdraw from the business and leave Agnes Mason's fate in the hands of a hostile jury, come the Midsummer Sessions. That would be prudent, would it not?'

'A hard man, Giles Cobbett,' Hester observed, on a sudden. 'I knew his late wife Mary… as did my mistress.'

'I remember,' I said.

'Mary Cobbett was so small,' she continued. 'Some called her a mouse. She feared her husband – I've heard it said he beat her as if she were an errant servant.'

'I recall hearing that too,' I said, as the memory surfaced.

'The daughters were very alike… three peas in a pod. I expect they are still - the two that remain, that is.'

We were distracted by some chair-scraping from Childers, who stood up and excused himself. For once he was unwilling to be part of the discussion, though his disapproval was plain. But he left the table courteously, saying he had matters to attend to. Hester waited until he had gone before turning to me.

'I intend to go to the funeral at Ebbfield tomorrow,' I said, to forestall her. 'Beyond that, I've made no firm resolve. Yet you saw the condition of Edward Mason. Had you seen his mother, you might…' I left the sentence unfinished.

'I'd like to come with you,' she said. 'If you're willing.'

I took another drink. 'I doubt you'd be welcome, any more than I will. Cobbett's not a friend.'

'Yet, despite the circumstances of Susanna's death, I say we should both go. You as a landowner and a former Justice, I to represent my mistress. You know she would have gone.'

'That's true,' I allowed.

'And while you're exercising your powers of observation, I might have opportunity to speak to others about the girl's tragic demise. For there are clearly some loose ends to be tied – do I hit the mark?'

In spite of everything, I allowed myself a smile. Little escaped Hester - which thought engendered a pang of unease.

'Well, mayhap the ride would suit you,' I said, somewhat quickly. 'And the mare could do with the exercise.'

'Good, then it's settled.'

Soon after, we rose from table, she to go to her embroidery and I to my private parlour to attend to my letters. Only then did I realise that no mention had been made of the household accounts. It was unlike Hester to forget - had I seemed so preoccupied, I wondered, that she thought it best to postpone the matter?

That night I went to my bed in poor humour, and sleep was slow in coming. Nor was it improved when I awoke, with the prospect of the funeral ahead. It struck me then, that the last one I had attended was that of my beloved Margaret.

***

The day was fair, however, and the ride pleasant enough in morning sunshine: across the river at Worcester, then southward towards the village of Kempsey. I rode Leucippus, Hester her chestnut mare Althea, the two of us in sable attire, our hats bound with black silk. A little north of Kempsey we turned aside on the lane to Ebbfield, Giles Cobbett's manor. There were no other travellers, which caused me to wonder if we were somewhat late for the ceremony. And on reaching the house, which was shaped like an H, its imposing entrance flanked by two-storied wings, we found the place all but deserted. We crossed the moat by its narrow bridge, entered the courtyard through its covered arch and drew rein. I recalled that the chapel, built a century ago by Cobbett's forefathers, stood at the rear of the house. I was about to dismount when a servant appeared from somewhere, stumbled towards us and made his bow.

'Your pardon, sir…' the fellow was aged, white-haired and stooped. 'If you seek my master, I fear I must dissuade you. The house is in mourning, and I'm loth to trouble him.'

'We come to attend the funeral,' I said.

At that, the man looked surprised. 'Is it so? I… in truth, sir, we did not expect mourners from outside the family. Might I know your name, that I can convey it?'

I told him, naming Hester as waiting-woman to my late wife.

'Justice Belstrang… of course.' He peered at us both. 'I must tell you that the service is almost over – it was my master's wish it be done early. Yet you may attend the burial, if it please you. I cannot think there would be objection…'

His eyes fell, his agitation plain to see. Perhaps he thought we were ignorant of the circumstances of Susanna Cobbett's death, and feared it would fall to him to inform us. To put him at ease, I lifted a hand.

'Pray, do not fret,' I said. 'We are aware of the tragedy that has befallen your master and his family. We're but here to offer condolences. And we'll wait at the graveside, if that's fitting.'

The old man's relief was evident. 'By all means, sir… Master Justice. If you'll dismount, I'll have your horses cared for and convey you to the place.'

It was done, a stable lad arriving to lead our mounts away. Thereafter Hester and I followed our guide through the doors of the house, where all was still and silent, with not even a servant to be seen. Soon we had passed through the hall to a rear door which led to the gardens. Some distance away stood the small chapel surmounted by its cross, with the Cobbett family's arms. Looking towards it, I bent my ear for any sound, but heard nothing.

'Are many mourners come?' I enquired of the servant.

'In truth sir, you are the only ones not of the household,' was his reply. 'Apart from Master Humphreys and his wife, who are tenants. The family wished for privacy, in view of...'

He broke off. Likely he had known Susanna Cobbett all her life; it was a tragedy for everyone. Seeing him fighting tears, I laid a hand on his arm.

'I pray you, leave us and go your ways,' I said. 'We'll find the grave.' But as the old man bowed and turned to leave, I stayed him. 'One moment: the service. Who is conducting it?'

'That's Parson Woolland, sir,' the other answered. 'Thomas Woolland, from Kempsey.'

The name was unfamiliar to me. I watched the old man walk away, head down, whereupon Hester and I took the path to the chapel. We would not enter, but walked past it. I was curious: something felt amiss here, though I could not have named it. Soon we stood in a grassy area, with a fence and a view of fields beyond. There were no headstones; members of the family were interred in their vault at the church in Kempsey. But a short way off was a freshly dug grave, with a mound of earth beside it. Nearby stood the solitary figure of a labourer, spade in hand, regarding us without expression.

Just then, Hester took my hand. 'They're coming out,' she murmured.

I turned to see the chapel doors open, and drew breath: the burial of Susanna Cobbett was about to take place.

FIVE

The first person to emerge from the chapel was a gaunt, bony woman swathed in black. She was followed by two slight figures: Giles Cobbett's surviving daughters, heads bowed in grief. The woman, I surmised, was their nurse. After waiting for them to draw level, she proceeded to shepherd them forward. Then the parson in his surplice appeared, walking with stately gait, followed by the coffin borne on the shoulders of four servants clad in black druggett. The unmistakeable figure of Cobbett himself followed: handsome and imposing, gazing straight ahead. Close on his heels came a stout, middle-aged man whom I guessed was his tenant, Humphreys, guiding a woman who walked somewhat hesitantly. They were followed by a handful of Ebbfield servants, men and women, dressed in everyday garb.

There had been no time, I realised, with Susanna's funeral following so hard upon her death, to fit them out in mourning attire. And in truth it was a sorry, almost ragged procession that filed towards the grave. Hester and I had drawn aside, but as the only bystanders we were conspicuous enough. There were glances in our direction. Jane, the elder daughter, a pretty girl of perhaps fourteen years, looked sharply at me. While the younger one, whose name I recalled was Alison, barely raised her head. Both were stricken with grief, their eyes wet with tears. Neither of them knew me; then, I had not set eyes on them since their mother was alive, when they were small children. The only person to recognise me was Cobbett himself, who stopped in surprise.

'Belstrang... Good God sir, is it you?'

'It is, sir,' I answered. 'I'm come with my late wife's companion, to offer our sympathies.'

Cobbett glanced at Hester, but barely acknowledged her. 'Indeed? Well then, I must bid you welcome.'

And yet, though the words were spoken smoothly, I stiffened: there was suspicion in the man's cold grey eyes. Hester saw it too, and lowered her gaze.

'I pray, come into the house after... later,' Cobbett added

28

quickly. 'A funeral table is prepared.' With a nod he moved off, leaving us to follow as we wished.

We waited, our attention now on Abel Humphreys and his wife. For a farmer, I thought, he was an odd sort: heavily-built and fleshy of face, with little trace of the permanent sunburn common among men of the land. He saw us, but looked away quickly, while his wife… his wife, I now realised was blind. Her sightless eyes stared ahead, though there was no mistaking the tears which ran from them.

It struck me then, with some force, that of all those present, Mistress Humphreys and Cobbett's two daughters were the only ones who showed any sign of real sadness, apart perhaps from the servants. But the thought receded as the burial service began - for it was the most discomfiting I have ever attended.

At first matters proceeded as expected. Parson Woolland, a grim-faced man, intoned the words while the mourners stood with bowed heads. The coffin was then lowered into the earth, to the muted sound of sobbing from the Cobbett girls. Their nurse, meanwhile, stood like stone - a hard woman, I decided; then her master was a hard man, as Hester had said. Cobbett, for his part, stood with the air of one whose main concern was to get the business over with. I turned to Hester, the two of us standing at the rear, and caught her glance.

'I never saw a father so unmoved,' she whispered.

But we were diverted, for there came a restlessness among those present: an air of anticipation, or even of unease. Its cause, I realised, was the parson who, having closed his prayer-book, now drew himself to full height and glared round at what was become his congregation.

'Evil was done to this innocent maiden,' Woolland said, in a voice of doom. 'An evil that many might fear to confront - yet I shall not shrink from my task.' He paused as if daring anyone to speak, but there was only silence.

'Madness comes in many forms,' he went on. 'Some may mock, while others weep at the plight of the afflicted. The heaviest burden is borne by the families, who are oft driven to torment by the trial God has seen fit to place upon them - and yet…' This with a fierce gaze at every person in turn. 'Yet this trial, this cruel visitation came not from God, whose purpose is beyond our understanding. It came from a servant of Satan, albeit one in human form: the form of a woman who dwelt but a short way from where we stand, before she was taken. I name her not – I have no need, for you know of whom I speak.'

He stopped, closed his eyes and muttered what I assumed was a prayer. The listeners were still, heads bent low. Cobbett appeared impassive, while beside him the shoulders of both his daughters shook with silent sobbing…

And then I saw something: something that sat most starkly with the occasion. Abel Humphreys turned his head to Cobbett, who returned his gaze - and to my astonishment, the two exchanged private smiles.

The smiles were gone almost at once, both men assuming an attitude of close attention as the parson opened his eyes. But I had seen it, and would not forget.

'Yea, you know full well of whom I speak!' Woolland thundered, his voice loud on a sudden. 'That one, that cursed demon, now faces due process of law - and if justice prevails, she will go to the pit that is prepared for her. I need say nothing further, yet I will remind you of those words from Exodus, in the eighteenth verse of the twenty-second chapter, that show us the will of God in such matters: 'Thou shalt not suffer a witch to live.'

Whereupon, to murmurs from some of the servants, he ended his sermon – for such it was. It was no eulogy, no plea for mercy or understanding for the girl who had committed the grave sin of self-murder, but a sermon, which he now concluded with an amen before turning to walk away. He was followed by Cobbett, Humphreys and his wife and the servants, who dispersed in silence. Soon only the two sisters remained at the graveside, standing close together and a little apart from their nurse, who appeared ill-at-ease with their grief. The labourer, meanwhile, stood ready to do his work.

'I'd like to go,' Hester said. 'Yet, if you wish to tarry at the house-'

'I don't,' I said.

I was still struggling with the picture in my mind: of Cobbett and his tenant, whose wife had stood beside him in ignorance, smiling over the bowed heads of the other mourners. After a moment I offered Hester my arm, but as we began to take our leave a female voice called out. I looked round to see the older of the Cobbett daughters coming towards me.

'Sir... might I know your name?'

I told her, and was about to summon some words of sympathy, but her response cut me short.

'You were the Justice, in Worcester?'

'I was. I... we knew your mother in happier times,' I began - but I was at once arrested by the look in her eyes. There was more than grief: there was nervousness, even fear. Hester saw it too, and caught her breath. By instinct both of us were moved to try and comfort the girl – but almost at once, we were challenged.

'Jane! What are you doing?'

I looked up to see the nurse, skirts swishing about her as she hurried towards us. Without checking her stride, she took Jane Cobbett by the shoulders and almost thrust her aside.

'In God's name, sir, have you no shame?' she demanded of me. 'Troubling my poor charge in her grief, at such a time? I pray you, go to the house and attend your father!'

The instruction was for Jane who, without a word, turned about and obeyed. But as she went, she threw a look over her shoulder which I will not forget: that of a soul in anguish. I had barely noted it before the nurse faced me again, but quickly I recovered myself.

'I had not the least intent to trouble your charge, Mistress,' I said, in my magistrate voce. 'She came to me... I believe she wished to speak.' Whereupon I gave my name, adding that I had some acquaintance with the Cobbett family. Such explanations, however, seemed of little concern to this woman.

'There was small need for you to come here... sir,' she answered. 'This family is in torment, if not one of their own making, and in need of privacy. I would have thought a man of your rank and education would have understood.'

'Might we know your name, Mistress?'

Hester spoke up, her eyes peering into the other woman's.

Another moment followed, before the nurse nodded briefly. 'Eliza Dowling. Master Giles' daughters have been in my care since their mother passed.'

'Your care?' Hester was taut as a wand. 'Well, it appears to me they will need more than mere discipline in the days ahead,' she said. 'They will need understanding.'

'Do you presume to teach me, Madam?' Eliza Dowling retorted. 'I'm grateful, but I fear my duties call me. If you'll allow?'

Whereupon, with a look of severity, she turned and called out to the younger sister who, I now saw, had been watching our exchange open-mouthed. But she came meekly, and was soon swept away towards the house. I watched as both figures disappeared from sight, before glancing absently at the grave.

The labourer was at work already, shovelling earth so quickly, he seemed in haste to have the dead girl's remains hidden from sight, for ever.

***

We did not speak for some time on the ride homewards, each of us busy with our thoughts. Finally, as the spires of Worcester's churches came into view, we slowed our mounts and walked them at gentle pace.

'Those poor girls,' Hester murmured. 'Who will they turn to now, with no older sister to be their confidante?'

I made no answer; the particulars of the burial and its aftermath were yet fresh in my mind.

'Something was wrong back there,' she added. 'More than the tragedy of the death.' She glanced at me as we rode. 'Humphreys, for one thing – the tenant. He made my blood run cold. For that matter, so did the parson.'

I nodded. 'I wouldn't like to be one of his flock when he's in full flow, spouting fire and damnation.'

'And what of Cobbett?' Hester asked. 'You saw his demeanour as I did.'

But I was thinking of Agnes Mason, who was likely unaware of the strength of feeling gathered against her. If ever there were a hopeless case, I reflected, hers was one.

'I had a notion we might take our dinner in Worcester,' I said finally. 'But if it please you, we'll go home directly. I've some business this afternoon, that will not wait.'

Hester threw me a questioning look, but said nothing.

Nor did she query my request, back at Thirldon, for Henry the cook to put some cakes in a pouch, along with a stoppered flask of ale, and bring them to me after we had dined. Though from her expression, she guessed where I intended to go.

***

Two hours later I stood once again in the gloomy Guildhall cellars, before the door of Agnes Mason's cell.

My arrival had not gone entirely smoothly, for in the entrance hall I had been confronted by an official who told me the prisoner was now forbidden visitors. On learning who I was, however, the man relented and called Sergeant Lisle. After I had surrendered my sword, the sergeant accompanied me downstairs to the chamber at the end of the passage. Key in hand, he paused at the door and regarded me.

'Might I enquire as to what's in the bag, Master Justice?'

'Cakes and ale,' I answered. 'Is the prisoner now forbidden such comforts?'

'Not by me, sir,' Lisle said. 'But I have to ask. I'm also obliged to search you, but let's take that as done, shall we?'

I sighed and gave him my thanks, whereupon he unlocked the door and stood back. This time I had no need to adjust my eyes to the gloom, for there was a small rushlight burning. In its feeble glow, I entered the cell to see Agnes Mason rising from her pallet in surprise. As the door closed she stood up, smoothing her skirts hurriedly, but greeted me warmly.

'Master Justice... once again, you cheer me.'

Somewhat awkwardly I held out the bag; I had forgotten how disarming her smile was. She took it and thanked me.

'A costrel of ale and some sweet cakes,' I said. 'Better than prison fare, I suspect. Do they feed you properly?'

She nodded and set the pouch aside, her smile fading. 'I make no complaint, sir. But the jailer is harsh... he dashed my porridge to the floor this morning.'

At once, I pictured Burton's smirking features. My anger must have shown, for Agnes lifted a hand. 'I pray you, let's not speak of him. I'm eager for any news you bring – do you know aught of Edward and Isabel?'

'They are well,' I answered, hoping it was not an untruth. I hesitated, then added: 'I fear my other news is not pleasant.'

'And yet I would hear it,' she said. 'It's unlikely to be worse than any I have imagined, here in this place.'

Seeing her somewhat dispirited, I let my gaze wander the grimy chamber. 'If only we could sit,' I said absently.

'Well, why should we not?' Agnes replied. 'The bed's none too clean, but it's better than cold stone.'

Whereupon, somewhat to my embarrassment, she sat herself down on the pallet, in the corner of the cell. Drawing her knees up to her chest, she looked up. Will you join me, sir?'

I did so - most clumsily, I should add. A man of my station is unused to such a posture, and given my years… but no matter. The two of us sat side by side, which could have put certain thoughts in my head, had my news not been so grim. For I felt obliged to acquaint Agnes with all that had passed since our last meeting: *In primis*, Boyd's report of the inquest, and *secundus*, my own account of the funeral. I made no effort to sugar the tale, for there was little to gain by it. After I had finished, I leaned back against the rough cell wall and let her ponder the matter in all its starkness.

'Well, I should thank you,' she said after a moment. 'Even if my fate appears sealed. Might I ask you sir, as a man of the law, what your advice would be? To await trial and try to gather some defence? Or to keep silent, putting my faith in the hands of the Lord?' She paused, her eyes on the floor. 'Either way, I fear the result will be the same.'

I failed to summon a ready reply, whereupon she added: 'Or might there be another way? You carry a poniard… perhaps you could mislay it, when you rise to take your leave? Or would you deny me the chance to cheat the gallows, while I may?'

I turned sharply, uncertain if she was in earnest. But I could divine little from her expression, and a chill stole over my heart.

It was a feeling I knew would not lift, unless I could find some means to save this woman's life.

SIX

My remedy, on this occasion, was not to fall back on a pious-sounding attempt to dissuade Agnes from such a desperate act as she had hinted at. Nor did I assume my lawyer's manner and speak of her defence at trial – a defence, I knew, which would carry little weight against the testimony of Giles Cobbett, let alone public opinion. Instead I put rank aside and spoke as I would to any friend in need.

'I'll pretend I never heard that,' I told her, in a severe voice. 'And I resent having my time wasted with foolish talk. I wish to help you, but I cannot do so unless you help me. I need to hear something new – anything you can think of, which may be of use.' And thinking fast, I seized the first notion that came to mind.

'Cobbett's tale of your cursing him, for instance - telling him his firstborn would perish. I know it's a lie, but in the absence of witnesses, if he swears to it-'

'My word is worthless,' Agnes broke in.

'Well then, the gold,' I persisted. 'The so-called Offa's gold. Are others aware of his desire for it? Or of his notion to have you divine its place, by conjuration?'

She thought for a moment. 'It's likely Humphreys would know,' she said finally. 'They're close, those two… more than is common between landlord and tenant.'

I frowned as the memory arose of Cobbett and Humphreys, exchanging smiles at the graveside. 'Will you say more?'

'You have seen him, and his wife, you say… that poor woman. To my mind she's never viewed him as he truly is, being blind from childhood. Some still wonder why he wed her, for there's precious little warmth in the marriage. They say he visits women of the town… in some ways, I might say Sarah Humphreys is as much a prisoner as I am.'

I pictured the man, as he had walked by Hester and I: his wife in tears, while he betrayed no emotion.

'The pool,' I resumed. 'Your son spoke of the old rumours. It's not somewhere I intended to visit again, but is there aught I might find if I did? Those birds, hung in trees – do you think they were placed to scare intruders? If Cobbett believed the gold was hidden nearby…'

I broke off, for Agnes was nodding. 'You might ask Ned Berritt about those,' she said.

I recalled the name, as I recalled Edward Mason describing the man. 'How so?' I asked.

'I cannot be sure,' Agnes answered. 'But Ned's sharp-eyed, and wiser than many would credit. I'd not call him a friend, but nor is he our enemy. He has no affection for Cobbett, or Humphreys either. Humphreys caught him rabbiting on his land once, and offered him a choice: either he would report him, or he could take a beating then and there. Being Ned, he took the beating, which Humphreys enjoyed dealing out, so he swore. It meant bruises and a cracked rib, but it spared him from being arrested.'

I pondered her words. It might pay me to visit Humphreys on his farm, I thought, and try to probe the man for some clue to this conundrum. For so it was become, the more I learned of the matter. 'I should go soon,' I said to Agnes. 'I'll do what I can… though I fear it may not be enough. It would be an untruth to tell you otherwise.'

I turned to her, and our faces were suddenly close – whereupon I drew back, lowering my gaze. Had I betrayed my feelings? The notion brought unease, which was only compounded when Agnes laid a hand gently on my arm. But when I forced myself to meet her eye, I saw only gratitude.

'You have my deepest thanks,' she said.

With an effort I got to my feet, grunting a little. Agnes too rose, a good deal more nimbly than I had. But I confess that her next words came as a disappointment.

'I pray you, sir: feel no need to come here again,' she said. 'Unless there are tidings you wish to bring. Though you warm my heart with your presence, there's only sadness when you're gone. You understand me, I think.'

With a quick smile of farewell, she faced the wall and stood motionless. And though I had an urge to reach out and turn her towards me, I did not.

Instead, with heavy heart I stepped to the door, threw it open and got myself out into the passage. Had the insolent Burton been waiting just then, I believe I might have struck the man down merely on impulse. But it was Lisle who stood nearby, regarding me without expression. With barely a nod, I walked past him to the stairway.

The next day, I resolved, I would go again to the Witching Pool, unhindered by the presence of another. There I would hunt about - for what, I did not know. But the notion of doing nothing was too grim to contemplate.

***

The following morning it rained heavily, yet I was undeterred. Having passed a restless evening and a night of broken sleep, over breakfast I told Hester of my plans. She looked somewhat askance, but passed no remark. Thankfully Childers had supped and was elsewhere, which spared me a warning about venturing out in the rain. But it proved to be only a May shower, which eased off as I rode down to Powick village.

After crossing the bridge, I followed what was now a muddy track, and a short while later drew rein at the edge of the trees. There I dismounted, left Leucippus to graze and walked through wet grass until once again the wood closed about me. Birds squawked angrily at the intrusion and somewhere an animal scurried off. I soon reached the pond, where I halted, allowing the woodland sounds to flow about me.

And quite soon, any unease I may have felt melted away. For this time the Witching Pool seemed utterly peaceful, even welcoming. Had I been a man of fanciful nature, I might have put it down to the fact that I bore neither fear nor ill-will. Whatever the cause, I found the glade tranquil and the water still, save where rainwater dripped from the trees. It might even be a place for contemplation, such as the ancients sought. And once again, I found it hard to believe that young Susanna Cobbett had come here to do what she did.

The thought was uppermost in my mind, when the peace was shattered.

From out of nowhere came the sound of something hissing towards me, prompting me to whirl round. I ducked, then let out a gasp: only inches from my head, an arrow was embedded in

37

the trunk of a tree, its shaft quivering.

'Who's there?' I shouted, reaching for my sword.

There was no response. I stared into the trees, yet saw no-one - whereupon, to my dismay, came the same sound I had heard on my last visit: a bark of laughter. But this time it came not from across the pool; it was uncomfortably close. In alarm, I turned about to see a ragged figure emerge from behind a great oak - and the next moment recognition dawned.

'By heaven, I've seen you!' I exclaimed. 'You were up before me, when I was magistrate.'

'I was, Master Justice Belstrang... sir,' came the growled reply. 'You levied a fine on me, one I was hard-put to pay. Do you recall how much it was?'

I was too stunned to answer. Instead I watched as the man came forward, stepping through the undergrowth as surely as only one accustomed to the wilder places can. His clothes were drab and patched, his hair roughly cropped, the beard tangled like briars. In his hand was a short bow, on his back a quiver of arrows fletched with hawks' feathers. And at last the name I had heard from Edward Mason, and only the day before from Agnes, struck home: Edwin Berritt, known as Ned, poacher and occasional thief... how could I have forgotten?

'You know me now?' he demanded, drawing close enough to make me flinch. 'Then, you sentenced so many poor bastards in your time, why should you?'

I struggled to gather my wits. But when I raised a hand to point to the arrow in the tree, I was cut short.

'Calm yourself, Master. If I'd wanted to split your skull, I could have done so with ease. Let's call it a woodman's welcome, shall we?'

'How long were you observing me?' I asked, drawing a breath.

'Heard hooves, a while back. Like that other day you came... it's a fine horse you have.'

Our eyes met, and I was at pains to discern the man's demeanour. I saw resentment, but no real anger... whereupon, as the memory arose, I barked a question.

'Those birds hung about the trees. Are you the-'

'What birds be they?' Berritt broke in.

I looked about, seeking the sights I had observed before: the dead crow and thrush. But even as I did so an opinion was forming... somewhat ruefully I faced the poacher again.

'You removed them, did you?'

'Don't know what you mean, Master Justice.' Berritt's stare was as blank as any I have seen. Despite the differences in our rank and station the man was unafraid, even disdainful. I decided to abandon the topic.

'Well... no matter.' With a wry look, I tried to summon some shreds of authority. 'Now that we meet, I would have words with you. I've talked with Edward Mason, and...' I broke off, unwilling to speak of Agnes, but Berritt was ahead of me.

'About his mother?' He regarded me through narrowed eyes. 'That's why you come digging, is it? I heard you'd too much time on your hands, since you lost your place as magistrate. Do you mean to have a part in hanging the witch now?'

'By heaven, I have no such intent,' I retorted, with some heat. 'I'm trying to help her, and moreover-'

'Why, has she come into money?'

'What? You insolent rogue...' I drew myself up, hand on my sword. The man's nerve was more than I could bear - but once again, I was wrong-footed.

'Easy, sir - 'twas a jest.' There was mirth in Berritt's eyes, though he was still alert. It struck me that, in the absence of witnesses, had I drawn sword I would likely have come off worst: the man wore a skinning knife at his belt that looked sharp as ice. With an effort, I reined in my temper.

'See now... we appear to have made a poor start,' I allowed. 'Be assured that I mean no harm. I seek intelligence, nothing more... and as for the woman you call a witch, I believe she's wrongly accused. Perhaps you're unaware of the particulars, but were I to tell you...'

I stopped myself. Berritt's expression had changed, along with his manner. He let out a sigh, and looked aside.

'There's naught you need tell me,' he said quietly. 'I know what's been done, and it chills me as it would any man.' He faced me again. 'You seek intelligence, you say? Well, mayhap

I could aid you - but I'll not set foot in any court of law.'

'I understand,' I said, after a moment. 'And as I once fined you - though I'll admit I do not recall the sum – I would pay you something now. Would a shilling serve? A day's wage, for many.'

I waited, half expecting him to demand more, but it seemed his mind moved elsewhere. 'Agnes Mason is a good woman,' he said. 'There's some hereabouts have reason to be grateful to her... she'd do no harm, not even to a cockroach.'

He had relaxed somewhat, and my spirits lifted. If he had knowledge I could use, even a scrap of evidence...

'I share your opinion,' I said. 'Though, along with her family, you and I seem to be the only ones. Can you tell me anything – something you've seen or heard?'

'I might...' Berritt glanced about warily, as if there were anyone near, when it was obvious there was not. I had thought him a fearless man; could I have been mistaken?

'Whatever you tell me, none shall know from whose lips it came – I swear it,' I told him. 'But if you can help Agnes in her plight...'

'You've seen her, then?' the other broke in.

'In her prison cell. She's calm, but afraid... everything stands against her.'

'I'd wager crowns on that, right enough,' Berritt snorted. He seemed to be debating with himself.

'The night Giles Cobbett's daughter is said to have come here,' I ventured. 'Would you know anything of that?'

He hesitated, and I found my gaze drifting to his bow, which was still strung. That was how he took rabbits, as no doubt he could take any other creature he chose. I must have betrayed my thoughts, for the man bent the weapon's tip to the ground and unstrung it. Without a word, he then stepped to the tree with the arrow and, after some tugging, removed it.

'I would,' he said, turning to face me. 'And don't ask me why I was out that night. Yet hear this: I never poached on Mason's acres. They're poor folk.'

'However, we're on the edge of Humphreys' land, are we not?' I countered. 'Have you any scruples on his acres?'

Berritt merely busied himself tucking the arrow away in its quiver. Whereupon I reached for my purse, opened it and drew out a silver shilling. 'Take it,' I said. 'Whatever you tell me, it's yours.'

I proffered the coin, which was accepted in silence. Stowing it in a pocket, my informant spat on the ground, then spoke.

'If that maid came here, I didn't see her. I was some way off... but if she did, she wasn't alone.'

'Do you mean you saw someone?'

'Not close... only shadows. But there were men – two or three. They carried no lights, the way they were crashing about. Then, there was moonlight enough to see by.'

'But this is important,' I blurted. 'You must-'

I caught my breath, for Berritt's blank look was back. He would not testify, he had said, and though he could be compelled to it, I had agreed to keep his anonymity.

'Have you any inkling who they might be?' I asked instead. But for answer, he merely shook his head.

'Then, did you hear their speech?' I persisted. 'Any noises... a splashing, for instance?'

'I've said I was some way off,' Berritt answered. 'If there was, likely I wouldn't hear it, for the trees muffle such sounds.' He paused, then: 'I disappoint you, but that's all I can say. Save for one thing, if you'll hear my opinion.'

He eyed me, then spoke words which would change my perception of the entire matter.

'If you seek to know how that maid came to drown herself, Master Justice, I'd not be poking around here, for the water keeps its secrets. I'd be searching for her swain – her beau, if you will. His name's Howell Rhys, from the Welsh borders - and he was so smitten with love, he would swim across the river to meet her, night after night.'

And as I stared, the poacher slung his bow across his back and turned to go. 'Now I'll bid you good-bye. Likely we'll not meet again - for I'll hear you long before you see me.'

With that he was gone, melting into the trees and leaving no trace but the sound of rainwater dripping into the pool.

SEVEN

Back at Thirldon I took time to reflect on what had passed, seated in the garden after a good dinner. I could have been a hundred miles from the Witching Pool, with its secrets. For that matter, I could have been a hundred miles from the gloomy cell where Agnes would, in my mind at least, be sitting hunched on her rough pallet. Having spent the best part of an hour in grim contemplation, I heard footsteps on the gravel path: Hester and Childers were advancing upon me.

'Master Justice, we would speak with you,' my steward said. Whereupon, despite misgivings, I gestured them both to take vacant stools at the old table.

'I'm troubled, sir – as are we both,' he continued, wearing his gravest expression. 'Touching upon the business of the witch… I mean Mistress Mason,' he added. 'If you'll heed the advice of those who are most concerned for your safety…'

'My safety?' I echoed tartly. 'Why, what kind of danger do you suppose I am in?'

'Not bodily danger, perhaps,' Hester said. Sitting upright, she faced me across the board. 'But there is a threat to your standing. We thought you should be aware of it.'

'Indeed?' I frowned. 'What are the gossips saying, then?'

'It's more than a matter of mere gossip, sir,' Childers said. 'There's troubling talk in Worcester… Mistress Hester bore the brunt of it this morning.'

I turned to her. 'I didn't know you were in the city today.'

'Only at market. Where I was accosted by someone known to us both, if slightly: the wife of Justice Standish.'

I stiffened, as she went on somewhat quickly: 'She was harsh. She said you do yourself no good, taking up the case of the witch – those were her words. The town will turn against you, she said. Her husband is most displeased that you visit Mistress Mason, taking her food.'

I remained silent.

'I pray you, tell all of it,' Childers urged, in some agitation.

Whereupon Hester drew breath and added:

'You remain in her cell longer than is fitting, it's said, so that folk wonder what passes between you. They speak of the woman's charms, which are of diverse nature.'

'My God – do they think she's bewitched me, or seduced me?'

On a sudden I wanted to bang a fist down in anger. Instead I sat upright and, as I would do in my magistrate days, placed my hands flat. Childers looked wary, but Hester was calm.

'It appears that some do,' she replied.

'And what of you?' I eyed each of them in turn. 'For if you have any suspicions about my motives, perhaps now is the time to voice them.'

'Sir, I swear… you know better than that, I hope,' Childers said. 'But you must compass how the matter's viewed by the common sort - even by your equals.'

'Like Justice Standish, you mean?' I snapped. 'Well, by the Christ, it's time I went to see him - lay the entire matter before that slippery old goat. I have new evidence…'

I stopped, seeing how both of them stared. There was a cup of sack on the table, still unfinished, which I now took up. Having drained it, I set it down and gave a sigh. 'Let me tell you what's passed, since we last spoke,' I said.

And I told them what I had learned, from Agnes and from Ned Berritt. By the end of it, both were silent. Such silences, however, never lasted long where Childers was concerned.

'This will do no good, sir… forgive me, but I must say it. You intrude on ground that's best left to others.'

'And who might they be?' I retorted. 'Do you think Giles Cobbett would probe any further? From what I see, his only desire is to put the matter to rest, along with his daughter.'

'This young man… Susanna's swain,' Hester said. 'Surely if Berritt knows of him, others do too?'

'I'd wager on it,' I answered. 'If, by Berritt's account, the fellow swam across the river to keep tryst with his beloved, he would likely have crossed Humphreys' land. I mean to question him too – after I've spoken to Standish.'

'Master Justice, no!' In his agitation, as so often, Childers had forgotten his place. 'It would be folly to go to Standish. You and he are known rivals. At the least, he would refuse to hear you - he thinks first of his own station, and such favours as he may garner from men of rank and power.'

'Ay, men like Cobbett,' I countered. 'So, your counsel remains the same as before: I should step away from this whole affair and look to myself.' He made no reply, whereupon I faced Hester. 'Would that be your advice, too?'

'If it were, would you heed it?' She answered. 'For it appears you're resolved to play Sir Galahad and rescue this poor, wronged woman, or perish in the attempt. I speak only of the death of your reputation,' she added. 'But then, you seldom give much thought to that.'

It was a pretty speech, and I confess I was chastened. More, once again I suspected Hester had divined more than she would say. After some thought, I nodded.

'I'll not go to Standish... not yet,' I said. 'I need more evidence. But I'll go to Humphreys first thing tomorrow. I want to look that man in the eye, and see what moves him.'

I summoned a defiant expression, but there was no further argument. Both wore looks of resignation, mingled with relief.

***

There was a wind blowing up the Severn the following morning, somewhat damp for May and bringing clouds. Having passed once again through Powick village I rode southwards, but instead of veering off as before I continued along the lane to Abel Humphreys' farm, which stretched to the river's bank. Passing through fields, I slowed Leucippus to a walk. I had no wish to frighten the dozen or so cows, of our red-and-white Midlands breed, which grazed nearby. Soon the farm came in sight, at the end of the track.

Riding into the yard, which was muddy and cluttered, I reined in and looked about. It was quiet, thought there was a labourer slouching in the barn doorway observing me. I was about to hail him when the door of the farmhouse was thrown open, and the portly figure of Humphreys himself appeared.

'Good morning, sir,' he called. 'Are you looking for me?'

'I am.' Leaning forward in the saddle, I nodded a greeting. 'May I dismount?'

'But of course!' With an eagerness that took me by surprise, the man came forward. He wore a plain jerkin and heavy boots, though there was no dirt on them. 'I knew you at once… you were at Ebbfield. I pray you, come inside and take refreshment.'

Not having expected such a welcome, I hesitated before getting down. Breezily, Humphreys called to his man to take good care of Leucippus. Then we were walking to the house, my host speaking rapidly.

'I confess I did not know you, on that sad morning – I beg your pardon. Cobbett set me aright later… as if I'd not heard of Justice Belstrang! It was kind of you and your servant to attend. Neighbours should stand together – and we're neighbours, are we not? Give or take a few miles…' he chuckled. 'But let me bring you to my dear wife, who will be honoured to receive you - as are we both.'

Still talking, or I might say chattering, the man ushered me inside. I found myself in a bare, sparsely-furnished parlour with the remains of breakfast on a table in the window. The farmers I knew were all up by sunrise, and out in the fields by now… I turned to Humphreys, to find him still smiling.

'I pray you, sir, forgive the clutter… we are at present without a house-servant. My wife is obliged to attend to everything as best she can. You, er, you might have noticed her condition, when you last saw us…'

'I did,' I said. 'And I have no wish to trouble her. I marked her grief at the burial.' I paused, then ventured: 'It affects people in different ways, does it not? Grief, I mean.'

I was keen to note the other's reaction. But nothing seemed to shift Humphreys' grin; and naturally enough I recalled the smile he and Cobbett had exchanged, only two days earlier.

'That it does, sir… but let's not speak of sad things. I have a jug of good ale…' this with a wave of his hand towards the table. 'Or would you care for a cup of sweet sack?' He was still smiling, but raised an eyebrow when I shook my head.

'In truth, I've not come to pay a neighbourly call. If you'll spare me a little time, I would like to ask you some questions.'

'Why, of course, if you wish.' Humphreys scarcely blinked. 'Will you sit yourself down?' He moved to the table, waited until I had taken a stool, then sat across from me.

'Your wife,' I said in a casual tone. 'Will she come, or…?'

'Presently, sir, presently… she's about some trifling matter,' came the reply. 'Now, I confess I'm intrigued by these questions of which you speak – how can I aid you?'

I was about to fall into lawyerly mode, but delayed it. I was beginning to find Humphreys' smile somewhat annoying, and had a mind to disarm him. 'Do you have children, to help you work the farm?' I enquired, to which the other quickly shook his head.

'I fear the Lord has not blessed us in that regard, sir. But we have our health, and our wits. A man must be grateful for his portion.'

To startle him I changed the topic. 'You'll have heard of one Howell Rhys? A young man from the Welsh border country? I gather he was in the habit of venturing out by night, to swim across the river. The shallowest place I can think of is on your land, is it not? But a short way from Tait's Crossing?'

My response, however, was a look of puzzlement. 'Rhys, you say? Nay, Master Belstrang, I've not heard the name. Has he done some crime, or…?'

'He was, I'm given to understand, the lover of Susanna Cobbett,' I replied. 'He would meet her in secret… perhaps because her father forbade her to see him?'

'Indeed?' Humphreys appeared shocked. 'Well, I know naught of that, but if Sir Giles ever took such action, I'm certain he only had his daughter's interests at heart.' The man's smile had slipped briefly. 'He is – was, a devoted father to poor Susanna,' he added. 'And if it please you, I prefer not to speak of that business… such a tragedy.'

'It was,' I agreed. 'Yet it's my belief the matter is far from over. You might say, the ripples in the pool have not ceased.'

Humphreys blinked owlishly, but his recovery was swift. I knew that the man's cheerful bonhomie was a mask, though I was in ignorance of what might lie beneath it. I decided to leave the matter of Howell Rhys.

'You mentioned crime,' I said, assuming my bland look. 'And there might well be crimes yet to be uncovered. Sending an innocent woman to the gallows, for example... would you not call that a crime?'

He blinked again, but this time made no reply.

'Or are you convinced,' I persisted, 'as you testified at the inquest, that Agnes Mason is to blame for Susanna Cobbett's apparent madness, and her death?'

I waited, believing I had dented his easy manner at last. But at that moment there was a sound from the doorway. I looked round to see Humphreys' wife walk into the room. Her sightless eyes stared straight ahead, but her steps were sure, as of a woman who knows every nook and cranny of her home. Wearing a plain black frock, she stopped a short distance away with hands clasped before her - and I knew she had heard what had passed in this room. I would have spoken, had not Humphreys seized the moment and almost leaped from his stool.

'My sweet... pray, be at ease. It's Justice Belstrang from Thirldon, come to visit. You'll recall he was at the burial?'

'So I was told.' Sarah Humphreys turned towards me. She would have said more, I believe, had her husband not taken her arm and guided her to a stool - which guidance, I saw, was neither desired not necessary.

'Now don't distress yourself,' Humphreys said, with mock severity. He resumed his seat, his forced smile turned upon me. 'My wife is – indeed we are both, still somewhat raw with mourning, sir,' he said. 'And I'll not speak of that woman you have named, not in my house. I believe you'll understand.'

I made no reply, but deliberately faced his wife, who sat between us. I sensed she was aware of my gaze, and was proved correct.

'What do you want of us, sir?' She asked sharply. 'Surely you haven't come to offer sympathy, as you did at Ebbfield? That was your reason for attending the burial, was it not?'

She waited, the picture of icy calm, but her husband at once broke the silence. 'The Justice... I should say the former Justice... is seeking answers to some questions,' he said quickly. 'I'm uncertain yet as to his interest in this... the recent business. Perhaps he will tell us.'

Forcing another glassy smile, he eyed me. So, thinking it best to make what capital I could, I sallied forth.

'You spoke at the inquest of the dead girl, touching her condition of mind,' I said, falling into magistrate mode. 'You implied she was frail, perhaps susceptible to the influence of others. Would you care to tell me how you know that?'

'Because we're close neighbours of Giles Cobbett, as well as his tenants,' Humphreys replied. 'I've known his daughters all their lives. She's… she was a quiet girl, prone to fancies.'

'What sort of fancies?'

'I assure you, I'm not privy to their substance.' The man was maintaining his smile with an effort.

'What about the legend of Offa's gold?' I persisted, as the notion occurred. 'Then, she'd not be alone in believing there was some truth in that old tale, would she?'

'Pah! Stuff and nonsense!'

It was Sarah Humphreys who spoke. She was scowling; more, her fists were clenched, her upper body taut with anger.

'There's no gold, and never was!' she added. 'Only a prize fool would think so – though we've no shortage of those.'

Whereupon a dead silence fell. My gaze flitted between the two of them… and then I saw it, with stark clarity.

This woman loathed her husband with a bright hatred, from the very depths of her being.

EIGHT

I quitted the farm soon after, with questions still unanswered. I had grown weary of the couple; an invisible cloud of something distasteful seemed to hang over the two of them. I had meant to probe further, but lost my appetite. And though Abel Humphreys attempted to play the cheerful host to the very end, the sham was thin and tawdry. Making a brief farewell, I put Leucippus to the trot as I left the yard, with no appetite to return ever again.

As I rode I turned the matter about, but could not come at any conclusions. A visit to Doctor Boyd in Worcester, I knew, would lift my spirits, and within the half hour I was back in the city, on foot and making my way to his house. But on this occasion, I was disappointed: my friend was absent, his servant informed me, and not expected home until the evening.

I decided to take dinner at the Old Talbot to mull things over. And it was there, surrounded by townsfolk – some of whom glanced in my direction – that I came to a resolve: one that flew in the face of what I had told Hester and Childers the day before. I would throw caution aside and go to Justice Standish - the legal authority, as well as a chief source of my unease. I was reminded starkly of it when I realised that some of the looks I had attracted were less than friendly, if not downright hostile.

It was time enough, I thought, after fortifying myself with two or three mugs of ale. I would beard my old rival in his den – his fine town-house close to the Corn Market – and have matters out with him, for better or worse.

It was not the first time I had dismissed the advice of Hester and Childers; I hoped I would not regret it.

***

To begin with, my visit to the Justice's house went cordially enough. Standish, grizzled and unsmiling in his black gown, received me coolly but courteously, given my former rank. I was admitted to his private closet, lined with books and hung with portraits, and invited to take a chair facing him across a table piled with papers. But the moment I began to state my business, the man grew defensive.

'By God, so it's true,' he grunted. 'I did harbour a forlorn hope that you came for some other cause, but I see I was mistaken.' He sighed dramatically. 'Once a meddler, always a meddler, Belstrang. Even in retirement... have you naught to busy yourself with, on your estate?'

'I have,' I replied, keeping my temper. 'But when a family in turmoil comes to beg my aid, I'll not refuse them. Would you?'

'Doubtless the family you refer to is that of the witch, Mason,' Standish said. 'May I offer you some advice on that score?'

'There's no need,' I replied. 'You would merely be adding your voice to those of others, who have already advised me to avoid the affair like the plague.'

'Then they were wise to do so. Surely a man of your experience can see that the case against the woman is strong? Besides, I cannot and will not discuss it. You know well enough that I won't preside at the trial. It's a capital crime, and a matter for the Quarter Sessions.'

'Then will you discuss the inquest into Susanna Cobbett instead?' I enquired. 'Since that's now a matter of record. I gather your sympathies were entirely with the girl's father, with little thought for the deceased.'

At that, Standish's anger rose quickly. 'I don't recall you being present on that occasion,' he retorted. 'Is this mere hearsay, or...'

'My good friend Doctor Boyd was there,' I broke in. 'He reported the substance to me – and I should add, he was most dissatisfied with the way the business was conducted.'

Standish paused, sitting rigid in his high-backed chair – and then exploded.

'How dare you, Belstrang! Do you forget to whom you speak? If you mean to accuse me of some malpractice, then lay it forth now – indeed, I demand that you do.'

'If you wish,' I answered. Though a little startled by the man's reaction, I confess to some satisfaction at having ruffled his feathers so easily. 'For one thing, I heard that no-one examined the body of the deceased, to confirm whether or not she died by drowning,' I continued. 'Moreover, that pool is shallow and not easy to find in the dark. Given the distance from Ebbfield too, it seems unlikely that-'

'Enough, sir!' Eyes ablaze, Standish cut me short. 'I'll not have you coming to me with these theories, not to say accusations. Do you suggest I had motive in despatching the affair without proper scrutiny? It's intolerable!'

'Is it so?' I fixed him with my bland look. 'Then you're not interested in hearing fresh evidence? If I had any, that is?'

'What evidence?' the other demanded. 'By God, Belstrang, it appears you've been poking your nose in, further even than I was told. Visiting the witch in her cell for private conference - and that's not all, some say.' A sneer appeared. 'Then, it's no secret you've taken your late wife's woman as your bed-maid, out at Thirldon... perhaps you were seeking a little diversion here? Some small reward, for promising to take an interest in this woman's case? Even one who consorts with the devil? Shame upon you!'

Well now, as Childers might have said, that blew the cask open. In truth, I see now that I had gone to Standish for a fight, one that was long overdue. Why else had I fortified myself at the inn? Resisting the urge to get to my feet, I leaned forward and lifted a hand.

'I've heard it said there are many sorts of witches,' I snapped. 'Men as well as women. Yet Agnes Mason has never harmed anyone, and as for driving a maid to madness, the notion is preposterous. Yet, along with most of this town, you seem to have condemned her before she even comes to trial. You question my motives – what of yours? Will you be hosting the Assize Judge here in your house, as you've done before? It would be a fine opportunity, would it not, given the King's interest in such cases, to lift your reputation? For heaven knows, you could do with it.'

'Good God - you vile old rogue!'

It was Standish who got up. 'Always a blunderer - intemperate and stubborn, as was your father!' he cried. 'Why in God's name should the fate of this wretched woman matter a jot to you? Then, you never could be dispassionate, which is why you were unfit to be a magistrate! I said so then, as I say it now…'

He stopped himself – but too late. In the taut silence that followed we stared at each other, while in my mind memories flew up and rearranged themselves into a clear pattern.

1612: those meetings of the City Fathers… a letter from the Attorney General in London… the mutterings in corners, at the Assize Sessions… the Mayor too is displeased, it was said. Then that gloomy day when I was called before the Council and asked, most politely, if I would step down from my place as magistrate. I could plead ill health… the burdens of office were becoming too much to bear… for the good of the city, it was for the best - was it not? And seeing how they were resolved, on that occasion Robert Belstrang set aside his stubbornness and, to his shame, acquiesced.

I had regretted it ever since - more deeply, I realised, than I ever allowed myself to think. And standing before me was one who had been instrumental in bringing it about: a man who had appeared sympathetic at the time, even as he stepped so readily into my shoes.

'Well now, that's clarified matters somewhat,' I said finally. 'I believe now, that I always knew you were one of those who contrived to have me ousted.'

I was about to go, but decided to take a parting shot. 'As for the evidence I spoke of, I'll keep it to myself. I'm no longer confident in its being heard dispassionately.'

And I left him, still on his feet. He was no longer looking at me, but down at his cluttered table.

***

I walked after that, for the rest of the afternoon. I neither knew nor cared which way, but allowed my legs to carry me where they would. In the end I found myself by the river, watching two boys fishing from the bank and half-wishing I could join them. Years fell away: the pair could have been Boyd and I, laughing and exchanging jibes as we cast our lines, two frisky lads without a care in the world. Naturally enough, and in need of a friendly ear, I at last began making my way back through the city towards his house. If he had not yet returned, I decided, I would wait.

In fact, Boyd was at home. And though weary from the day's business, he was pleased to have me join him and take a cup of sack. There I spilled my tale, telling all that had transpired since our last meeting. It was a relief to unburden myself, even if my friend was somewhat subdued by it all.

'I'll admit I've heard mutterings myself, in the city,' he said, after some thought. 'They say the King likes to be kept informed of such cases. Which suggests to me that a man of stern, if not fixed opinions might be sent to try Mistress Mason – even some notorious witchfinder. Had you considered that?'

'In truth I had not,' I said, with a frown. 'But given James's loathing for supposed witches, it could be so.'

'Have you read his book, *Daemonology*?' My friend enquired. 'It's poorly written, in my view. More to show off his learning than to shed any new light on such matters.'

'I have not,' I answered absently. I was mulling over the day's events, particularly my visit to Humphreys' farm. I would have spoken further of it, whereupon by some instinct Boyd forestalled me.

'At the risk of letting fancies get the better of me, I'd say there's another sort of witchery going on behind all of this,' he said. 'Giles Cobbett, for example.' Seeing he had caught my attention; he added: 'They say his tenant Humphreys is an idle fellow, who's far in arrears with his rent. Yet Cobbett allows him to continue, with little sign of censure. Odd, don't you think, for a landlord who seems eager to squeeze his poorer tenants, like the Masons?'

I frowned, as a picture formed of the smiling farmer with his scowling wife sitting beside him. 'It is… but they're tight together. I thought it might have had something to do with the business of Offa's gold.'

'That's a myth,' Boyd said scornfully. 'Half the country folk in England tell such tales, yet precious little treasure seems to come to light.'

'Yet, after all that's occurred,' I said, 'I still can't fathom why Cobbett's so set against Agnes. To accuse her of such a heinous crime, punishable by death? She pays her rent - why would he hate her so?'

'Only he can answer that,' Boyd replied – whereupon, seeing my expression he frowned. 'You're not thinking of confronting him? That would be unwise – especially at this time.'

'Likely it would,' I agreed. But I took a drink and allowed myself to compass the notion. Whatever might be the cause of Cobbett's false accusations against Agnes, I realised, I was not going to uncover it by avoiding the man. Though I had no relish for another visit to Ebbfield…

'By the Lord, Robert.' Boyd was frowning at me. 'I know you're not one who shirks a risk, but…'

'But what?' I broke in. 'I seem to have few other choices in the matter of gathering intelligence, which I promised to do.'

'Yet what use would it be? The case is set for the Assizes… you'll only bring further opprobrium on yourself.'

'So speaks the man who disapproved of the hurried inquest into Susanna Cobbett's death,' I countered. 'What was it you called it – a sham? Or was it a comedy?'

Boyd opened his mouth, then closed it. He generally enjoyed an argument, but this time the stakes were somewhat high. He took a pull from his cup, then eyed me.

'This Welsh lad, Rhys… the supposed suitor of Susanna Cobbett. Do you have evidence that her father knew of his visiting her? Or that he forbade her from seeing him?'

'I do not,' I admitted. 'That, too, is something Cobbett himself might answer.'

My friend paused a while, then let out a sigh. 'Well then, if you propose to go to Ebbfield,' he said finally, 'you'd be well advised to take along a witness.' And when my I raised my brows, he added: 'Someone he can't bully – who's not without influence in this city…'

'And has a good eye, as well as an open mind,' I finished. A welcome feeling, of mingled hope and relief, was upon me. 'Not to mention one who is a true friend – the kind a man is most fortunate to have.'

The other put on his disapproving look. 'You read far too much into the offer, Robert,' he retorted. 'Call it a professional interest in a case of self-murder… call it idle curiosity, or what you will.'

'I call it loyalty,' I said. And with that I lifted my cup, saluted him and drained it.

'Now I'll return to Thirldon. But if I were to call upon you about ten of the clock tomorrow, would you be free to take a short ride with me, out to Ebbfield?'

For answer, Boyd too raised his cup and drank off its contents, before setting it down with a look of resignation. But I knew him too well: he was a man of enquiring mind – he is so still. And I would swear there was a spark of excitement beneath his sober expression, even as he strove to hide it. Whether it was a rash decision on the part of both of us, would only be proven on the following day.

But neither of us could have had an inkling of what would unfold.

NINE

Ebbfield was still a house in mourning. And as Boyd and I rode out from Worcester under a blue sky, I confess I had misgivings as to what now seemed a bold, if not rash course of action. In truth I had few expectations of learning much, and more of finding my presence unwelcome. I should add that I had said nothing, back at Thirldon, either about my meeting with Standish or of my further intentions. I had no desire to hear further doubts expressed by Hester or Childers.

We were both wary as we approached the manor, slowing our mounts as the house came into view. But no sooner had we crossed the moat than we heard noises: stamping hooves, the barking of dogs and raised voices. Passing under the arched gatehouse, I was surprised to see seven or eight horsemen gathered in the courtyard, with servants milling about and several dogs off the leash. And there was Giles Cobbett on a fine coursing-horse, in conversation with others: men of his own standing, to judge from their clothes. Whereupon their business was at once plain: this was a hunting party.

I reined in, Boyd doing the same beside me. I confess I was at a loss for words: did Cobbett truly mean to entertain guests so soon after his daughter's burial, and in this manner? There was a restlessness about the man, as if he were eager for the chase - and at once Hester's words at the graveside came to mind: *I never saw a father so unmoved...* My eyes moved across the group, to settle on one of the horsemen. For a moment I wondered if I were mistaken - then saw that I was not.

Close to Cobbett, his gaze now upon Boyd and I, was Thomas Woolland, the parson who had conducted the funeral. He had swapped his vestments for hunting attire, though his demeanour was as I remembered: stern and forbidding. And the next moment, having caught the man's eye, Cobbett himself turned in the saddle and saw us.

For a moment he appeared confounded. Then, even from some distance away, I saw a flicker of anger cross the man's features, to be replaced by a look of bemusement. After murmuring a few words to those nearest to him, he shook the rein and eased his horse forward, to halt but a yard or two from Boyd and I. As if sharing my unease, Leucippus gave a snort and tossed his head.

'Belstrang?' Cobbett eyed me, his gaze far from friendly. 'What's this – were you hoping to join my hunt?'

'No... in truth, sir, I've always been a fishing man first and foremost,' I answered, summoning a faint smile.

'What of your friend?' He looked sharply at Boyd. 'Your face seems familiar, sir... do you have business here?'

'Not as such, sir,' the doctor answered. He gave his name and station, to which Cobbett barely nodded. Without troubling to conceal his impatience, he faced me again.

'Well now, if this is another sympathy visit, I'm most grateful,' he said, in a flat tone. 'But you see I have guests, and our quarry awaits. Perhaps we might postpone our conversation for another day.' He raised his brows. 'I assume it was a conversation you desired?'

'It was,' I answered. Glancing past Cobbett, I found the eyes of every horseman upon me – especially those of Woolland. His expression was more than one of curiosity: it was one of plain hostility. Looking away, I was about to make reply to the master of Ebbfield, when my attention was caught by a slim figure on a pale-grey mare... and it was all I could do not to give a start.

Jane Cobbett, the only member of the female sex present, was also looking at me - as intently as she had done but three days ago, at her sister's burial. With an effort I turned back to the girl's father, realising he was addressing me.

'As I've said, though it pains me greatly, I fear we must leave it for another time.' Cobbett's voice was heavy with sarcasm. 'I beg pardon if your ride was wasted... then it's a fine morning, is it not?'

To his irritation, however, feeling a surge of Belstrang stubbornness, I failed to heed the rebuff.

'It is indeed. Yet I'll admit I'm surprised to see you venturing out to hunt, given the short time that's elapsed since your recent loss. Your middle daughter, too... I formed an opinion that she was most grief-stricken, and likely to remain in mourning for a time.'

At that, the man fairly bristled with anger. I had gone too far... but then, I have often found this a way to get at the truth. Beside me, I knew Boyd had tensed; his horse felt it, and shifted restlessly.

'I think I've heard enough from you just now, Belstrang,' Cobbett said icily. 'In fact, now I think upon it, I've seen and heard enough of you to last me a year. Whatever your business, I suggest you take it away with you - now.'

He jerked the rein harshly, then turned in the saddle to deliver his final words.

'I've heard things of late, about your sudden interest in my affairs,' he snapped. 'Ill-judged and meddlesome, some call it, even discourteous – which matches your reputation, as I recall. But I say this: if you truly intend to take up the case of that cunning-woman, you make an enemy of me. And I give you warning: that is something no man who knows me well would ever wish to do.'

He turned his back and walked his horse back to his companions. Words were spoken – seemingly a jest of some kind, for the response was laughter from the other men. The dogs barked and frisked, sensing the start of the hunt – and at once the word was given, for the party shook reins and urged their mounts forward, Cobbett in the lead. With barely a glance at Boyd or me they swept past in a body, causing us no small difficulty in getting out of their way. Then they were through the gatehouse, hooves pounding as they spurred across the bridge, the dogs racing ahead. One of the last to ride out was Woollard, who threw me a withering look as he passed.

But he was not quite the last: looking very small and erect in her side-saddle, Jane Cobbett was walking her mare in the rear, and I knew that her slowness was deliberate. She drew close to me, lowered her head and spoke.

'I pray you, sir, do not make haste. Ride as far as Tait's Crossing, then wait for me. Will you do so?'

I glanced at Budge, and nodded.

***

A half-hour passed, and no-one came.

We had said little on our ride to the crossing, which was where we now sat on our mounts, at the side of the road. The Severn glided past, its surface dotted with wildfowl, while the small wherry lay idle, moored to the bank. As a ferry-boat it was seldom used: an old tub, many called it, run by an ageing rogue called Dan Tait, who lived nearby and earned a few pennies for his pains. There was no sign of him today, which suited me well enough.

'Perhaps young Mistress Cobbett has changed her mind,' Boyd remarked presently. 'I regret I can't wait all morning... though I'm as curious as you. She appeared frightened.'

'And I will hear her,' I said. 'I must. Though of course, I've no wish to keep you.'

'The parson...' Boyd was frowning. 'I know some churchmen enjoy a hunt, but he's an odd fish, that one.'

I nodded, recalling Woolland's fiery speech at the graveside, and his denouncing of Agnes Mason. At that moment, however, we were alerted by the sound of hooves: Jane Cobbett appeared at last, riding towards us at pace. She reined, somewhat breathless, and threw me a look of gratitude.

'I knew you would wait, Master Justice. You have my thanks, for in truth there's no-one else I can talk to - if you are willing to hear me, that is?'

'I am,' I assured her. 'As is my good friend here, Doctor Boyd from Worcester. Though I confess we were surprised to see you ride to the hunt... was it at your father's bidding?'

The maiden shook her head. 'I had to beg him to let me come – I needed to get away from her, if only for a few hours.' She looked away for a moment. 'I speak of our nurse, Dowling.'

'Indeed?' I glanced at Boyd. 'Will you say more? Does she use you harshly, or...?'

'At times, but that's not why I'm here,' Jane said quickly. 'There are other reasons - my sister for one. She is deep in melancholy, and I'm afraid for her.' She gave a sigh. 'Then, that's not something I should trouble you with. I must speak of another... his name is Howell Rhys.'

I gave a start: a picture of Ned Berritt arose, standing by the

Witching Pool as he told me of Susanna Cobbett's swain. At once I told Jane what I knew, to which she nodded.

'It's true. They were much in love, though unable to meet save at an open window, for the house is locked at sunset. I would keep a watch for Susanna, while she stole down to the back parlour... he would wait for her, shivering when the night chilled him in his wet clothes. Those were hurried meetings, tinged with sadness – they could barely even kiss!'

She was close to tears, but checked herself. 'They planned to run away together. But now, with what's happened...' she shook her head forlornly. 'He must be broken... I know not what he'll do, for he adored her.'

'Your father, I would guess, forbade the two of them to meet?' I asked – to which an answer came, with some emotion.

'Forbade them?' Jane echoed. 'More than that – he only saw Howell once, but swore if he ever saw him again, he would kill him on the spot! And I believe he would do it, too...'

She trailed off, biting her lip. I caught Boyd's eye, and saw he would speak.

'I pray you will take heart, Mistress,' he said. 'Things may not seem so dismal in time. Howell Rhys will mourn, of course - and deeply - but he's young, as you are. Once the time for mourning is passed-'

'It will not pass, sir.'

Jane eyed him sadly, moving both of us to pity her. Turning to me, she added: 'There are secrets at Ebbfield. Yet I'll not say more... you are kind, to hear me spill my thoughts.'

'Now wait,' I said, seeing she meant to leave us. 'I wish to help, yet you've not told me how I can. Do you wish me seek out Howell Rhys? I pray you, speak before you ride off.'

'I cannot stay longer, for I will be missed,' Jane said. 'I'll say that I fell behind, my mare being out of sorts, though whether my father will believe me is another matter.' She managed a brief smile. 'But yes, I would be grateful if you could ask after Howell. He lodges at a farm beyond Clevelode, where he minds the flock. He's a gentle fellow, and I fear for him.'

'Yet, you say he and your sister planned to elope?' Boyd enquired. 'How could they do so, without money or means of support?'

His answer was a bleak look. 'When the urge to flee is strong enough,' Jane said, 'money may be of least concern. Susanna believed Howell would protect her with his life – and so he would have done, had he any notion of what was about to happen.'

She looked down, patting the neck of her grey mare. 'I'll take my leave,' she said. 'If you have news of Howell, I beg you to pass it in secret to our old servant – Matthew, that is, with the white hair. Do you know him?'

I assured her that I did. And though I would have put further questions, clearly this was not the time. She gripped the rein and turned her horse, to face the way she had come. Then, after favouring me with a faint smile, she rode away. I watched her urge her mount to a canter and disappear from sight.

It fell to Boyd to break my reverie. 'So, you mean to go down to Clevelode and seek this young shepherd?' he enquired. 'For you appear to have promised it.'

'I have,' I admitted. 'Tomorrow's the sabbath… like everyone else he'll be at church. I believe I'll find him.'

Boyd made no reply, merely shook his reins. Thereafter we rode back to Worcester, my mind busy with the events of the past hour. From seeking to find ways to aid Agnes Mason, I thought, I now found myself on a path which was likely to prove at best a distraction, at worst troublesome. I was still pondering the matter as we entered the city, where we parted, Boyd to his duties and I to return to Thirldon. At least, there I could collect my wits, even if I had to avoid Childers poking his nose in.

But there would be no peace that day.

No sooner had I left my parlour to go to supper, than I was called to the stable yard where I found some of the servants gathered. Childers was among them, as was my groom Elkins, who seemed to be the centre of attention. He made his bow when I approached, as did the others save Childers, who looked even gloomier than usual.

'What on earth's the matter?' I demanded. 'I was about to dine…' I paused, catching the grim look on Elkins' face. 'Now you make me uneasy,' I said, with an attempt at levity. 'Has the

King fallen sick in Scotland, or just got drunk and fallen off his horse? Speak up.'

'The King is well, Master Justice, as far as we know.'

It was Childers who answered. 'But there is grave news,' he added, 'terrible news, from Newland. A rider passed on the road, and gave it to Elkins as he exercised the horses.' He hesitated, then: 'There's been another drowning, at the Witching Pool. Worse, they say it's another self-murder... a dreadful act.'

I stared at him - then heard Elkins pronounce words that froze me where I stood. 'It's a young lad... a shepherd from Clevedon way,' the groom said. 'Drowned himself last night, they say. He was found this morning...'

He fell silent, for I was no longer listening, but gazing down at the cobbles. Finally, I lifted my head and looked round at the faces of my trusted servants.

'Who discovered him?' I asked. 'And how can they be certain what occurred?'

'An old woodman found him, sir,' Elkins answered. 'One who's often about there. I don't know his name.'

Berritt... who else would it be?

'Very well,' I said, with an effort. 'We must await further news. For now, I'll leave you to your work.'

I glanced at Childers, intending to say something about our supper; then I realised I had lost my appetite.

TEN

On the following morning I rode into Worcester again, as church bells rang out for the Sabbath. Having found a boy to hold Leucippus, I went straight to Boyd's house. I expected the doctor to be at church and was prepared to wait, but to my relief he had returned. Though surprised to see me again so soon, he quickly discerned my humour and proposed a walk in his small garden. There in the sunshine, strolling among his fruit trees, I told him of Howell Rhys's death. But then with hindsight, I should have anticipated his response.

'It's not unknown,' he said. 'The youth could not face the future without his beloved, so chose to end it as she did, and in the same spot. Likely he thought their spirits would meet, and hence they would be together for eternity.'

I was thinking on what Jane Cobbett had said the day before; the explanation sounded plausible. And yet:

'I'm not sure I believe that,' I said.

Boyd lifted an eyebrow.

'Though most would view it as you describe, I'm unconvinced. I think that someone like Rhys, who had the courage to swim the river by night and crouch under a window just to snatch a brief moment with his Jane - when he's been told by her father that he'd slay him on sight - was made of sterner stuff.'

'All men are fools when it comes to love,' the doctor murmured.

'But at the least,' I returned, 'such an incident merits a proper inquest, does it not?' I had stopped walking, and stood amid the buzz and hum of insects. My friend turned to face me.

'Unlike the one held for Susanna Cobbett, you mean?'

'I do indeed.'

He was silent for a moment, then: 'There was an incident of a different kind, this morning in the city. During the night, it seems, someone nailed a paper to the doors of the Minster, accusing Agnes Mason. Calling her a servant of the evil one, a

63

demon in woman's shape… you're familiar with the terms. And demanding her death by burning, no less. Many people saw it. If feelings were running high before, they will certainly increase now, when news spreads of a second self-murder.'

'By heaven…' I felt my heart sink. 'Would they accuse her of bringing about this too?'

Boyd merely shrugged.

'But it's absurd… utter nonsense,' I exclaimed. 'Even if such things were possible, how could she bewitch the youth from a prison cell? And for what motive?'

'Logic is often cast aside, when fear and superstition run unchecked,' my friend said. 'But still…' he grew thoughtful. 'I do wonder who would go to the trouble of writing that paper, and fixing it where half the city would see it.'

I looked sharply at him. 'Then, you'll agree there may be rounds for further investigation?'

'Perhaps,' Boyd replied. 'There often are, are there not?'

'Well then…' I drew a breath: a resolve was forming, one that would perhaps help me to move matters forward. 'Supposing I were to go to Standish, who will no doubt preside at the inquest? I could say I had an interest in the case, without specifying what. Hence I could observe the proceedings, as you did before. Standish knows he can't pull the wool over my eyes, as a former Justice…' then as a new thought occurred: 'And more, as a respected physician, you could offer to examine the body.'

'Are you serious?' Boyd was frowning. 'Suppose he, or someone else, refuses? I can hardly insist.'

'You might,' I told him. 'You could say you're writing a report about what you observed at the inquest of Susanna Cobbett - one you mean to send to the proper authorities. Standish is most touchy on the matter. If he thought someone were to accuse him of malpractice…'

'Robert, enough!' Boyd wore his exasperated look. 'Your feelings run away with you. Though I've said I will help you in this business, you know my powers are limited-'

'What about gathering evidence?' I said, cutting him short. 'That's all I desire. I told Standish I might have something new, but I didn't tell him what. It nettled the man… he's not invulnerable. Between us, I believe we have reasons enough to insist on your viewing the corpse. If he objects, I might throw in a few veiled threats. So - in view of your professed interest in matters of supposed self-murder, what do you say?'

Having made my case, I waited. I was asking a lot, perhaps, but I knew Boyd. At last, he let out a sigh and nodded.

'If you can arrange it, then I will do it,' he said. 'But if I'm satisfied the youth died by drowning, that's the end of the matter – and of your case. If indeed, you have a case?'

It was a question to which I had no answer. But on a sudden, I knew what to do next: I would go again to Newland Wood and try to find Ned Berritt.

I wanted to hear what he knew, before the news became widely known.

***

In the early afternoon I left the city once again and rode downriver to Powick. After crossing the Teme I followed the lane towards Humphreys' farm, before turning aside and walking Leucippus along the grassy track. The route was becoming familiar, I thought; but recalling my previous meeting with Berritt, it dawned on me that I might not find him, which meant a wasted journey. I had no wish to ride on to the Masons' cottage, having nothing of comfort to tell them; after what had now occurred, their fears would only worsen. Hence, my hopes had dwindled somewhat by the time I dismounted at the treeline. I ventured into the wood once more and made my way towards the Witching Pool, now the scene of another tragedy. But very soon, I was checked.

There was a shout, and two men came striding through the trees towards me. One of them held a pistol. I stopped in my tracks, hand on sword, and drew a breath.

'Who are you, and what's your business here?' The one with the firearm demanded.

'I might ask the same of you,' I replied, gathering my wits. 'Whom do you serve?'

They halted, observing my station from my good clothes and my basket-hilt rapier. Seeing I was not a man to be browbeaten, the forerunner of the two lowered his pistol, blew the charge off and uncocked it. 'I'm not obliged to answer questions, sir,' he said. 'We have orders to keep a watch – the wood is dangerous.'

'Do you mean the pool is dangerous?' I enquired. 'I hardly think so.'

The two exchanged glances. By now I had looked them over and seen a pair of lackeys, unaccustomed to the role of guards. 'I asked you who your master is,' I went on, summoning my official voice. 'This is the border of Cobbett's land – is it him you serve?'

'We're not at liberty to say, sir,' the second of the two answered. 'But we are ordered not to let any man pass. There has been a death… the body was only removed this morning.'

I regarded him briefly, then turned my gaze upon the other. 'Has anyone spoken to the finder of the body?' I asked him.

'I know naught of that, sir.' Nervously, the man fingered the butt of his pistol. 'But I can tell you there's no more to be done here.'

In spite of my resentment at being treated in this manner, I realised he was probably right. I would find nothing new – and Berritt, of course, would be nowhere near.

'The corpse – do you know where it's been taken?' I asked.

'To the church in Powick,' the unarmed man answered. But at a look from his companion, he lowered his gaze.

'Do you have an interest in the matter, sir?' The man was eying me suspiciously. 'I mean no insult, only-'

'That's as well,' I broke in. 'Or you may regret it. And like you, I'm not obliged to answer questions. Instead I'll leave you to your duties, superfluous as they seem. I can't imagine sightseers flocking to this spot just now, can you?'

I turned about and left them, retracing my steps. I was both disappointed and curious; why had those men been placed here? And why did they refuse to say whose orders they followed?

Still turning these questions over, I returned to Leucippus where he grazed. At my approach he lifted his head, ready for me to mount the stirrup. Instead I took up the rein and led him back along the track. At least I had learned where the body of Howell Rhys was, I thought; I needed to inform Boyd, before taking the bold step of confronting Standish again about the inquest.

I was pondering the matter, when Leucippus suddenly came to a standstill. At the same moment there was movement in the bushes beside the track. Turning sharply, I peered about – whereupon a bark of laughter almost caused me to jump out of my skin.

'Berritt... by the heavens, is that you?' I called.

For answer there came a twitch of branches, and the familiar figure of the woodman appeared. With a glance at Leucippus, who eyed him warily, he stepped on to the track and faced me.

'Why, were you expecting someone else, Master Justice?' He enquired, with that innocent look of his.

'Once again you catch me unawares,' I said with a sigh. 'Were you following me?'

He gave a shrug. His appearance was precisely as before: the same clothes, the quiver on his back, bow over his shoulder. But my feeling now was one of relief – he was here after all, and I was not about to waste the opportunity.

'In fact, I came looking for you,' I told him.

After a moment he nodded. 'About the Welsh boy, is it?'

'I heard it was you who found him. Is it true?'

'True enough.' Berritt turned aside and spat. 'A bad business... two lovers, bound in spirit now.' He eyed me. 'Did you seek him out, like I told you last time?'

'I would have done, had I the chance,' I answered. 'Now, will you tell me what you know? It's important.'

'I see that.' But he would not be hurried, I saw. With a glance to either side as if to reassure himself we were alone, he moved at leisurely pace towards Leucippus and began to stroke his neck. As a rule, my horse was loth to let anyone save myself touch him, but this time he seemed content.

'A fine steed,' Berritt said. 'What do you call him?'

I told him, then waited until he turned to face me.

'The boy was in the water right enough,' he said. 'Been there all night, to my reckoning... they'll be needing another shepherd at Rowden's now, eh?'

'Was that his master?' I asked. 'The farm where he worked?'

He nodded. 'Tom Rowden... like I said, it's a sorry business.'

I strove to rein in my impatience. 'See now, is there anything more you can tell?' I asked. Fumbling for my purse, I found a silver sixpence. 'Take this for your pains.'

He took it without a word, then: 'I said to you once, Master Justice, the pool will keep it secrets. But I've seen drowned men before, when the river's in spate... and that one didn't look right.'

'How so?' I demanded.

'The face,' Berritt answered. 'The colour wasn't what you'd expect. More, he wasn't dressed like you'd expect – he was muffled in a shepherd's cape. He'd been out with his flock – I don't believe he'd leave them untended.'

'What... do you mean he was abducted?' I said sharply.

'I can't say. But there were bushes broke and flattened, like there'd been a struggle of some sort. I saw Rhys, pulled him out on to the bank, then walked to Rowden's and told them. A constable was fetched, and the body was carried away. I'd done my part, so I stayed clear.'

Thinking fast, I took in his statement, then thought it best to tell him something he might not like. 'You know there will be an inquest,' I said. 'And from what I've heard, you'll almost certainly be called to give evidence.'

'Eh?' He frowned. 'No - I told you before, I'll not set foot in any court of law.'

'It's not a trial,' I said. 'It's an inquest, likely to be held in the old tithe-barn at Powick. You only need tell what you found-'

'I said no!' Berritt scowled. 'There's some could make trouble for me, if I'm stood up before the while village.'

'Someone like Abel Humphreys?'

At mention of the name he tensed. It was bold of me, I realised, given what Agnes had told of Humphreys' treatment of this man. But I would not lie to him: he was a witness.

'See now, I'll vouch for you,' I said. 'I can sit with you, if you wish, and escort you out. You only need describe how you found the body... there's no call to repeat all that you've told me.'

For a moment the man continued to scowl at me - then, to my surprise, he threw his head back and gave one of his barks of laughter.

'By Jesus, Master Justice…' he shook his head. 'When all's said and done, under your learning you're a rogue like me at heart – would you lie to a court, if it suited you?'

'I most certainly would not,' I answered hotly. But seeing the glint in his eye, I experienced a sudden urge to laugh. Stifling it, I drew breath.

'Though I might keep certain matters to myself,' I admitted, 'should they be of help to others.'

To that Berritt laughed again, a low chuckle. But the next moment he glanced about restlessly, as if eager to be gone.

'I told you how I wish to help Agnes Mason,' I said. 'And you know there are strong feelings against her in Worcester. Can you see that she might even be blamed for causing Howell Rhys's death?' And when he frowned again, I added: 'Anything else you can tell me might be of value – I pray you, speak it now while you can.'

'No more about the death,' he answered, after a moment's thought. 'But to earn my coin, I'll say this. You once asked about the dead birds… things set out to frighten folk away, you said. Well - in that, you were right enough. I was paid to do it, now and again. Make 'em look like witches' charms, or some such. It suited one man to keep folks away, so long as he thought there might be gold buried in the wood.'

I drew breath sharply, causing him to nod. 'Ay… you know who I mean. The same one whose own daughter drowned in the pool.' He grew sombre. 'It got to be a habit, hanging up crows and such. But I've stopped… no stomach for it now.'

I stared at him. 'Did you use other means to scare people away?' I asked. 'Like the creature that was said to live in the pool – big enough to send a wave onto the bank, I was told, and send folk running away in fear?'

'Ah… that.' Somewhat sheepishly, Berritt met my gaze. 'Well now… if you'll swear to keep it to yourself, I'll tell you.' And after I had nodded agreement, if against my better judgement: 'There was a great catfish in the pool once, as long as your arm. He was eating everything that moved, greedy bastard – it could have become a dead place. So I hooked him

69

and killed him, took him away. Had a few good suppers off him, after that.' He paused. 'Are you content now?'

Lost for words, I barely nodded. I might have said more about how this wild rogue, whom I had once fined, had been one of the chief causes of people shunning the Witching Pool for years; but I held my tongue.

And soon after we parted, Berritt vanished into the bushes whence he had sprung.

I would never see him again.

ELEVEN

Two days after my encounter with Berritt, I received a message by courier from Boyd: he had viewed the body of Howell Rhys, and asked me to attend him as soon as was possible.

Mercifully, the business had been easier to arrange than I feared. On my return from Newland I had sent a letter to Boyd, acquainting him with what I had learned. Then I sent another to Justice Standish with my request, offering to visit him and state my case, but to my relief there was no need. Perhaps to avoid another taut meeting, Standish agreed to Boyd acting as surgeon in the matter. Now, having received word I made haste to return to Worcester. I was unsure what to expect, but on arriving at the doctor's, I was both alarmed and intrigued to hear his findings.

'Unnatural?' I stood before him in his parlour, still perspiring somewhat from my ride. 'How do you mean?'

'I mean your friend Berritt was likely correct,' my friend answered in his phlegmatic fashion. 'The youth had been submerged, but there was very little water in the lungs – in short, his death was not by drowning.'

'Then, what did cause it?'

'Now we come to the nub of it,' Boyd replied. 'When I removed his clothing, down to the waist, I found heavy bruising about the chest and stomach...'

'What, do you mean he was beaten to death?' I broke in, my words tumbling over themselves in my eagerness.

'Robert, would you care to sit down and catch your breath?' My friend suggested. 'When I lay out the facts I'd prefer to do so in good order, if you'll allow.'

With an effort at calm, I seated myself. Boyd having done the same, he continued: 'As I said, there was severe bruising, but that's not what killed him.' He paused. 'In my opinion the lad was poisoned.'

'By the heavens...' At once I recalled Berritt's words: *The face... the colour wasn't what you'd expect...*

'I've seen it before,' the doctor nodded. 'The discoloured lips, the pallor... though since he'd been in the pond an entire night, it's difficult to be sure.' He frowned. 'Had I been able to examine the contents of his stomach, I could perhaps speak with more certainty. But since I was working under the eyes of others, who resented my presence, I thought it best to bring matters to a close - and to keep my findings to myself.'

'But this is important,' I said urgently. 'If Rhys was murdered – which is what you imply – it has a strong bearing on the case. Whoever had motive for such, I would-'

'Murder?' Boyd held up his hand. 'See now, I did not use that word. I merely said death was likely caused by poison. The deceased could have taken it by design, hence…'

'Then why would he go to the Witching Pool to drown himself?' I objected. 'It's absurd.'

'That, indeed, is the nub of it,' the doctor agreed.

We both fell silent. My own thoughts were running at speed: if Howell Rhys had taken poison, the verdict might still be one of suicide, given the whims of a jury made up of plain folk who simply wanted to get back to their day's business. His reasons would seem clear: the lad was distraught at the death of his beloved, and had no desire to live without her. At least, I reflected, there was no suggestion that he had been driven to madness by witchery.

'Who were these others, who resented your examining the corpse?' I asked. 'Do you mean they tried to prevent you?'

'No… they could not, once I showed my order from the Justice in his capacity as Coroner,' he answered. 'They could only throw me looks of disapproval. There was the constable from Powick – a dullard, who saw me as a meddling intruder. And some of the church people, who doubtless shared his opinion. Later came Rhys's master, the farmer… an angry man. He seemed more concerned that the shepherd had abandoned his flock, than the fact that he had lost his life.'

'Well, I believe Rhys was abducted,' I said. 'The bruising you found points to a struggle… he was dressed for the night-time, and would have been alone. But let's assume you're correct concerning the poison. Could it have been administered by force?'

Boyd was eying me uneasily. 'Robert, I pray you – rein in

these theories before they lead you astray. Whatever the means by which the poison entered his body, there's no proof of murder. Besides, who would wish the poor lad dead? Surely not Cobbett, if that's how your mind moves. With his daughter gone, he has no reason to pursue her forbidden lover.'

I gave a sigh, for he was right. Was I so eager to free Agnes Mason from the likelihood of conviction, I wondered, that I had grown obsessed with seeing Cobbett behind every evil that occurred? 'You read my thoughts too well,' I said ruefully. 'Some might call it witchcraft.'

'What with the fears and rumours that are about now, let's hope that word is not used at the inquest,' my friend replied.

'Yet you will present your findings, as told to me?'

'Of course. Unwelcome as they might be...' Boyd sighed. 'I'd not be surprised if our friend Standish tries to hurry matters along as he did before. A careless man, with a degree of idleness beneath his cloak of authority.'

'Well now, this time I'll be there to observe him and to make objection,' I said. 'And I confess that the more it discomforts him, the more satisfaction I shall feel.'

With that I stood and suggested dinner, to which my friend agreed. Yet he was as sombre as I, thinking on what lay ahead.

***

The following morning the inquest into the death of Howell Rhys, shepherd, took place in the old tithe barn at Powick, amid an air of some excitement. It was the second such procedure within ten days, and would no doubt be the talk of the village and its surrounds for a long time to come.

Along with Boyd, I arrived as men were setting out a table for the Justice. There was a handful of Powick folk present, among them a pinch-faced fellow whom Boyd pointed out as the constable. The jury of sixteen men were already seated, on benches at one side. I was observing them when my friend touched me on the arm. Turning, I was surprised to see someone I recognised, stepping in out of the sunlight: Thomas Woolland, the parson from Kempsey - and friend of Giles Cobbett. What, I wondered, was his interest?

But there was no time to think on it, for more people were

arriving. One was Abel Humphreys, dressed in the same garb he had worn when I last saw him. With him was a man who looked like another farmer, whom I would learn was Rowden, master of the deceased shepherd. Finally came Justice Standish, striding in with a harried look, a sheaf of papers under his arm. Ignoring everyone, he walked to his table and sat down heavily. And at once my hackles rose, for I saw that Boyd's suspicions were correct: Standish had the air of a man whose patience was short, and who wanted the entire affair despatched quickly.

And only then, as the Justice peered about the dusty barn, did I realise that there was no sign of Ned Berritt.

In the absence of stools, and with the few benches being already taken, Boyd and I were obliged to seat ourselves on straw bales covered with horse blankets. No sooner had we done so than Standish called the proceedings to order. An ageing, bird-like clerk then appeared from somewhere and announced the business in a bored voice, before seating himself close to the Justice. A hush fell, as all eyes went to him. Only now did he allow his gaze to wander over the small crowd... but if he saw me, he gave no sign of it. After shuffling papers about he murmured to the clerk, who stood up and called out a name I did not recognise: William Mount. With others, I looked round to see a figure come forward – and at once I stiffened.

He was the man with the pistol, who had confronted me in Newland Wood only three days earlier. And my surprise was confounded when, as the fellow stood before the Justice's table, he was named as the finder of the body of Howell Rhys.

I glanced at Boyd, and would have spoken had my friend not stayed me with a look which said plainly that we should wait. And so, I fixed my eyes on William Mount and prepared to hear his account. Having taken an oath, the man stood ready.

'I understand, from submissions received, that you came upon the deceased in Newland Wood,' Standish intoned, to which Mount nodded.

'I was exercising my dogs, sir. One strayed into the wood... I heard him barking, and found the dead person at the place they call the Witching Pool.'

There was a stir, which the Justice ignored. 'And what was

the condition of the body?'

'Floating in the water, fully clothed. I knew he was drowned, soon as I saw him. I didn't touch him... just went and reported it to the constable.'

Now my anger was rising, for the man was lying. Did he not expect to be challenged? And would not the constable testify that it was Berritt who had carried word to Rowden first? These thoughts flew about, even as Mount was being dismissed. Having sworn he had nothing to add, he was allowed to go. It seemed to me that the man quickened his pace as he reached the open doors of the barn, to disappear from sight.

Next to be called was the constable of Powick village. In a glum monotone, he stated that he had learned the whereabouts and condition of the deceased on the morning he was found, from William Mount. He had then gone down to Newland with a cart, in the company of other men. They had retrieved the body, swathed it and conveyed it here, to the church. The parish clerk had reported it to the authorities, after which the corpse lay untouched until the doctor from Worcester came to examine it. The constable looked round, and indicated Boyd.

'Likely that gentleman can tell you more,' he added. 'Meanwhile I stand to do my office, whatever it be.'

He waited, clearly thinking he was no longer needed... but I could no longer restrain myself. Standing up abruptly, I drew a breath and called out to Standish.

'Might I be allowed to question the constable, sir?'

There was a murmur of voices, and heads turned. I was aware of Humphreys and Rowden sitting together watching me, and of Woolland seated nearby. But I fixed my eyes on the Justice.

'Master Belstrang.' Reining in his irritation, he met my gaze. 'What, pray, do you wish to ask?'

'I have evidence,' I replied, causing another stir. 'Evidence that would contradict what we've heard up to now. If you will place me under oath, I would be glad to give it.'

A hush fell; beside me, I sensed Boyd's unease at my interruption. And when the answer came, it was no more than I should have expected.

'I might consider that, when I've heard from other parties,'

Standish said coolly. 'In the meantime, as a former Magistrate no doubt you'll be content to let me conduct this inquest in the proper manner. For the present, I ask you to wait.'

With an effort, I held my tongue and sat down. At least Boyd's testimony would be heard, I thought; as for Berritt, I was still puzzled by his absence. Yet that was as nothing to the dismay I felt when the next witness appeared - and I gave a start as the name was called: that of Eliza Dowling.

From somewhere at the rear of the watchers, she rose and made her way forward. She was still swathed in mourning black, with the air of a woman bowed in grief. It was enough to convince the clerk, who rose from his stool and placed it before the Justice's table. Murmuring her thanks, she sat down and faced Standish.

Tense as a pillar, I waited... to be confounded by her testimony. As accomplished liars go, I believe I never heard a better one. For this was a performance – as Boyd had described Cobbett's testimony, at his daughter's inquest. In a voice of sadness, dabbing at her eyes with a kerchief, the hard-faced nurse whom Hester and I had faced at the funeral won her audience over within minutes.

Firstly, she spoke of her late charge: her beloved Susanna Cobbett, from whose death, she claimed, she would never recover. Sadly, she related how she had watched Susanna fall into a despondency, an affliction of the mind which none could explain but which, in the light of what had since been revealed, she now understood. She appeared to wish to say more on that topic, but Standish interrupted.

'We are not here to speak of Mistress Cobbett,' he said, with impatience. 'The inquest into her death has already been held, in this very place. Kindly tell us what you know of the deceased, Howell Rhys.'

Mistress Dowling let out a long sigh. 'In truth, sir, I know little of him, save that he visited Susanna in secret... or so she believed. She was unaware that I had learned of the youth's attentions, by discreet observation. Naturally I reported the matter to my master, who ordered Rhys never to come onto Cobbett land again...' the woman paused, somewhat too dramatically. 'Yet the damage, I fear, was already done.'

'What do you mean?' Standish snapped. Whereupon, after giving another sigh, the nurse spoke those fateful words that no-one would forget.

'They were both bewitched,' she said, drawing a gasp from the watchers. 'Susanna, and Rhys too. It was he who urged her to take her own life, sir – I'm certain of it. Since they were forbidden, they would shed their earthly bodies, in the same manner and at the same spot, so that they could be together for all eternity. It was madness... they were driven to it, though of how that came about, I will not speak.' Slowly, she shook her head. 'May the Lord have mercy on them both.'

Having delivered her testimony, she fell silent... but for Robert Belstrang it was too much. In a moment I was on my feet again, causing heads to turn and Justice Standish to glare.

'Sir,' he growled, 'I have already told you that I'll consider any submission you wish to make-'

'And yet, I cannot and will not be silent,' I broke in. 'You, I and everyone here present have been lied to, sir... I demand that you let me give testimony-'

I stopped, or rather was prevented, by a hand gripping my arm: Boyd's. As I turned sharply to him, the doctor too rose and, in his voice of calm authority, addressed the magistrate.

'Master Coroner,' he said, 'I ask your pardon on behalf of my friend. He, like all of us here, is eager to see justice done... even if certain events have placed him under a strain. With your leave, I'll take the oath now and give the evidence I am come to deliver – at your own bidding, I might add. Evidence that may perhaps place the death of Howell Rhys in a clearer light... are you agreeable?'

There was a moment, as all eyes went from Boyd to the Justice. Whereupon, to general relief and a good measure of excitement, the man finally nodded. After dismissing Mistress Dowling, who rose and quickly vacated her chair, he beckoned the doctor forward.

Breathing hard, Robert Belstrang sank down on his straw bale and waited.

TWELVE

Boyd's evidence did not take long. In a dispassionate manner, he spoke of examining the body of Howell Rhys in the crypt of the church. His first task, he explained, was to verify whether the deceased had perished by drowning, as was supposed. And in that, he was obliged to report, the finder of the body had been mistaken. This caused another murmur of voices, which Standish quelled at once. Frowning at Boyd, he asked him to explain – which answer brought a collective sigh of dismay.

'By poison?' The Justice echoed. 'How can you know that?' Whereupon my friend repeated what he had told me the day before, about the lack of water in the lungs and other signs, as well as the suspicious bruising on the body. Hence, he added, it was his opinion that the deceased had-

But he got no further; raising a hand, Standish stopped him in mid-sentence. 'I do not wish to listen to more opinions, doctor,' he said frostily. 'I've heard enough of those from Mistress Dowling. Instead, I ask you this: could the marks you saw on the deceased's body have been occasioned by him forcing his way through a wood in the dark, perhaps causing him to fall – perhaps a number of times?'

Boyd eyed him stonily. 'Would not my answer to that also amount to an opinion?' He enquired.

Standish bristled. 'I pray you, sir, answer the question.'

'Very well, then: I think it most unlikely,' Boyd told him. 'It looked to me more as if he had been in a fight.'

There was another restless stirring among the watchers, to be silenced once again by the magistrate. 'Be that as it may,' he said, 'from what I see, there's no evidence at all that he was poisoned. But then again...' here he paused, and looked deliberately at the jury. 'Even if that were so, does it not seem likely, given what we know of the deceased's state of mind, that he could have taken it on purpose?'

'In which case,' Boyd demanded, 'why on earth would he go to the trouble of trying to drown himself?'

The response was a murmur and, to my quiet satisfaction, one or two stifled laughs - but Standish was having none of it.

'For the reason we have already heard,' he retorted. 'That in his troubled state, he wished to die at the same spot where his lover Mistress Cobbett perished. The poison – if indeed there was any – might simply have been a means to ensure that he succeeded in his aims.'

To that Boyd made no answer, and soon after he was asked to withdraw. For a moment he hesitated, then appeared to think better of it. But as he turned to walk back to his seat, he caught my eye, and I understood: my friend was more than dissatisfied - he was annoyed, which was rare for him. The matter was not finished, his gaze told me; my spirits lifted at the thought.

The next witness to be called was Thomas Rowden, master of the late Howell Rhys.

He came forward at a slow pace: a stolid man, walking stiffly. Having taken the oath, he fixed Justice Standish with a look of disapproval, as if he resented having to attend him. From the start, his evidence was that of a man who clearly had better things to do.

Yes, he confirmed, he was the farmer who had employed Rhys for more than a year. He had engaged him in time for last year's lambing, having had good reports of his work. No, he had no knowledge of when the boy, as he referred to him throughout, had made the acquaintance of Mistress Cobbett. He believed it was true, however, that Rhys had sometimes left the fields by night and crossed the river to keep tryst with the girl. Then, it came as no surprise to him.

'What do you mean by that?' Justice Standish enquired.

'What I mean,' Rowden replied, 'is that if ever a boy had his head in the clouds these past months, it was him. He was moonstruck… his mind not on his work. I had to chastise him, more than once. Lovesick, some might call it - that or bewitched, as Cobbett's woman put it.'

My hackles rising anew, I glanced at Boyd, who was tight-lipped. Once again, I thought, we were being told that those ill-fated lovers had been the victims of a madness caused by conjuration. And my view was only hardened as the Justice questioned his witness further.

'On the night in question, that of Thursday last by my reckoning,' Standish asked, 'were you aware that Rhys had abandoned his duties and gone elsewhere?'

'Not till the morning after, when he was found,' Rowden answered sourly. 'He stayed out with the flock some nights, so I wouldn't have known.' He shook his head. 'No shepherd I ever knew would have gone off and left 'em like that.'

Unless he was abducted, I wanted to say - and I might have done so, had Standish's next question not prevented me.

'You knew the deceased well – better than any other person present,' he said. 'In which case, I ask whether you are able to say that he was capable of taking his own life. Would you so swear?'

'Well now...' Rowden hesitated. 'He was sad enough and mad enough... so aye, I believe I'd say so. And now he's gone and done it, I hope to God he pays the price for his sins.'

He drew a breath, shifting on his feet. 'Am I finished now?' he demanded. 'For if I don't get back to my fields soon, I'll likely have sheep scattered from here to the Indies. Do you ken that?'

A moment followed which was tinged with amusement. I saw it on the faces of some of the Powick folk, who likely knew Rowden and his ways... but it was the face of Abel Humphreys that caught my eye. He too was smiling - quite broadly, and making no effort to hide it. And I knew at once that, if he too were called as a witness, he would tell a similar tale to those of Eliza Dowling and Thomas Rowden: that Howell Rhys had been bewitched like his lover, and driven to take his life – which in the end, meant by the actions of Agnes Mason.

But Humphreys was not called; nor was Rowden questioned further. After Standish had thanked the man sardonically for sparing his valuable time, he dismissed him. He then muttered something to his clerk, who dipped his quill and began writing on the papers before him. Along with Boyd, I watched Rowden walk stiffly away, to be followed by Humphreys, who had left his seat and moved to the doors. They left the barn without looking back.

I looked about: at Standish, at the jury who were already putting their heads together, at the plain Powick folk who spoke low among themselves. The verdict, I knew, was already decided. And it was no surprise to anyone when, but a few minutes after being directed to consider, the foreman of the jurors rose to announce that by their findings, Howell Rhys had taken his own life, by reason of being driven to madness.

With sinking spirits, I lowered my eyes. And though I burned with anger at the way Standish had guided the jury to that conclusion – a conclusion he himself appeared to desire – I no longer had the will to protest. Having barely listened as he pronounced the inquest closed, I turned to Boyd. But before I could speak a voice rang out, causing an immediate stir.

'Sir, we must conclude with a prayer!'

It was Woolland, the parson from Kempsey, on his feet in sermonising manner. Holding up a hand for silence, he fixed Standish with the same look I had observed at Ebbfield, when he raged against the evildoer who had driven Susanna Cobbett to madness. And as Standish blinked in surprise, he went on: 'I beg your indulgence, sir. We have heard testimony of wicked acts perpetrated upon two innocent young people, which drove both to commit the terrible sin of self-murder. Moreover, the mortal remains of one of them lies here yet, but a short way from this place. Like others, I am concerned to know how the body will be laid to rest... if there can be any rest, that is, for one who acted as he did.'

He paused, seemingly to reassure himself that he had everyone's attention, as if that were in doubt. Then:

'I for one would not bury this person in my churchyard, even were he of my parish,' Woolland went on. 'Nor, I understand, is the Powick parson willing. What then, is to be done?'

There was silence, until Standish at last found his voice. Furious at his authority being snatched away in such a manner, he too rose to his feet.

'Let me assure you, sir, that the deceased's father has already been informed, by letter,' he said loudly. 'For the present, the body will remain in the crypt of the church until it is claimed by his family. And I object to your imputation that I've given no thought to the matter. More, I dislike your addressing this inquest, which has already been concluded. The time is past for further submissions-'

'Like the one from the former Justice, you mean?' Woolland broke in harshly. 'You appear to have forgotten his request to be allowed to speak. Then, perhaps it would have delayed you, if you wish to make haste in going to your dinner.'

At that, jaws dropped; few had heard anyone address a Magistrate in such a manner. And though I confess to a sense of vindication at Woolland's words, I felt no warmth towards the man. He was on the verge of ranting, as he had done at Ebbfield that morning. With interest, I waited to see how Standish would respond.

'Master Belstrang?' Still fuming, the justice eyed me. 'I confess I had forgotten, for which I beg your pardon most humbly. Do you still wish to speak?'

All eyes turned in my direction; it was an opportunity, even if the inquest was over. I allowed my gaze to move from Standish to Woolland, and back to Standish.

'Would it alter the verdict, sir?' I asked, assuming my bland look. 'I think not, hence I will save my evidence for another occasion.' Seeing how that displeased him, I added: 'But I would welcome the chance to ask Parson Woolland what has brought him here – in effect, what his interest is in this case since, as he admits, the deceased was not of his parish.'

I turned to Woolland with raised eyebrows, and saw at once that I had put him on the defensive.

'You question my interest, sir?' He retorted. 'I'm a man of God, who goes wherever he is called. You yourself, I remember, were at the burial of the poor maiden who was driven to madness like the other one spoken of here - hence you will have heard my words at the graveside. We do battle with the evil one, sir, by day and by night – and I for one will not rest from my labours. Which is why…' he turned to Standish. 'Which is why, Master Coroner, I repeat my call for a prayer before we quit this place. So, with your permission?'

A moment passed, but it seemed there was nothing else to be done. With an effort, Standish recovered himself and gestured to the parson to do his office. I was somewhat surprised to see the fight go out of him so easily, though doubtless he was keen to get the business over. And so, at Woolland's bidding the entire assembly rose to their feet and bowed their heads, while he asked for a blessing on those present. He then murmured a short prayer for deliverance from evil, before ending with a loud amen. The company having made their response, conversation soon broke out, every man and woman turning to their neighbours.

The Justice, meanwhile, seized his papers and made for the doors followed by the clerk. I turned to Boyd, to find him gazing at the parson.

'I'm going after Standish,' I said on impulse. 'This inquest was a travesty, just as you described the one into Susanna Cobbett's death.'

'What do you intend to say to him?' My friend asked, turning to me. 'Or rather, what would it achieve now?'

'You saw it as clearly as I did,' I told him. 'He wanted a suicide verdict, so nothing more need be done. Now he can use both inquest reports at the trial of Agnes Mason, as evidence of her guilt – even though it was mere conjecture on the part of witnesses. And if the Worcester jury is of a similar bent to those men...' - I indicated the jurors, now talking among themselves – 'then the outcome is beyond doubt.'

'Well, if you are determined, I won't stay you,' Boyd said. 'But I confess my own suspicions lie elsewhere.' He nodded in Woolland's direction. 'A little too much righteousness there, perhaps... a little too much suppressed rage, for a man of God. In short, I wouldn't trust him with a bent farthing.'

'Nor would I, now you put it so,' I said, allowing my own eyes to stray towards the parson... whereupon I frowned. The man was now in conference with Eliza Dowling, the nurse from Ebbfield. As I watched, Boyd following my gaze, the two of them walked to the doors, talking low.

'What do you make of that?' he mused.

'I'm uncertain. But I would dearly like to confront Woolland at his own parsonage, and see how he behaves without a congregation to whip up.'

Dusting bits of straw from my breeches, I watched Woolland and Mistress Dowling leave the barn, as others were doing. A few looks were thrown our way, none of them friendly. I had been about to suggest that we take a cup of something restorative at the inn in Powick, but suspected we would not be welcome.

We got ourselves out into the sunshine, and made our way to where the horses were tied. The street was thronged with villagers, doubtless discussing the inquest. But having walked no more than a dozen paces, I stopped in my tracks.

Under the sagging eaves of a cottage, but a few yards away, three people stood huddled in private conversation: Standish, Woolland and Eliza Dowling. As Boyd and I drew near, the parson spied us and quickly turned his back.

'That notion you had, of bearding the man at his parsonage,' Boyd murmured, his eyes on the oddly-matched group. 'Might you and I go together? Tomorrow, say, after he's conducted his morning service?'

'I think perhaps we should,' I said.

THIRTEEN

The next morning I arose in sober mood. The cause of it was another taut conversation with both Hester and Childers the previous evening, which had led to some discord between us. In brief, Childers had allowed his concern for my welfare to get the better of him, and given vent to his fears once again.

'I know how you despise gossip, sir,' he had said. 'And you have oft ploughed a lonely furrow, yet this business of the witch – your pardon, of Agnes Mason – draws you ever deeper into a mire. There's been talk of dark shapes seen about Newland Wood, and cries heard - of something neither human nor animal. Moreover, there are calls for Mason to be removed from the Guildhall – from the city entirely, in fact – and lodged outside the walls.' He shook his head. 'It may displease you, yet I would fail in my duty not to warn you that you meddle-'

'With evil?' I broke in. 'Or mere superstition?'

'With popular opinion, at the very least,' was his reply. He sighed, and looked to Hester for support.

'Well, I thank you for correcting me,' I said. 'I thought I was doing my best to avert a perceived injustice, but even I may be mistaken.' I faced Hester. 'Would you care to give your opinion?'

I awaited her reply. I had already given both of them an account of the inquest, along with my views of it. And though I knew she was already displeased by my going to see Cobbett, as I had done despite giving assurances to the contrary, she had passed no remark.

'I heard in Worcester that Agnes Mason is refusing food,' she said, after a moment. 'Perhaps she means to starve herself, and so avoid trial.'

'Who says so?' I asked, somewhat too quickly.

'People in the market, and in the street…' She met my gaze. 'But as it's mere gossip, it shouldn't concern you.'

'It would concern me, if it were true,' I said.

She made no reply, and thereafter we had finished our supper in silence. But I was troubled: despite Mistress Mason's request not to visit her again, I was sorely tempted to do so. Then, I had nothing to report which could have encouraged her – quite the opposite. These thoughts were in my mind that morning, as I left Thirldon and journeyed into Worcester again to meet with Boyd. I found him in reflective mood.

'The town is now abuzz with talk of Mason's trial,' he murmured, as the two of us rode out of the city by Frog Gate. 'It seems there are some who claim they were healed by her, and would defend her. But the majority, I fear, are of the contrary opinion: that she's a witch, and must hang.'

I said nothing; and noting my humour, my friend sighed and changed the topic. 'See now, have you thought on how we might approach the parson this day?'

'In truth, I had not,' I answered. 'It wouldn't surprise me if he refuses to receive us. I can't forget that huddled conference yesterday with Standish and Dowling – especially as he and the Justice had been at loggerheads a short while earlier. Curious, was it not?'

Seemingly pondering the matter, Boyd gave a nod. Side by side, we rode down the Tewkesbury road on the three-mile journey to Kempsey, passing carts heading into Worcester. 'Moreover,' he said presently, 'what should one think of Abel Humphreys, in private talk with the nurse? Such a friendship also looks odd to me.'

I made no observation on that. Since Humphreys was Giles Cobbett's tenant, there was nothing odd about his knowing Eliza Dowling. But Woolland's apparent closeness to them was another matter. And why, I wondered, had he been willing to preside over the burial of Susanna Cobbett, yet refused to bury Howell Rhys, since both had been adjudged suicides?

I would have voiced the question to Boyd, even as the tower of Kempsey's church loomed ahead, but I was distracted by his next remark. 'Did I mention that he was also at the inquest into the Cobbett girl?' He enquired. 'Woolland, I mean.'

'You did not.' I turned to him. 'Had it slipped your mind?'

'I suppose it did,' the doctor allowed. 'What with Cobbett's performance, and Standish hurrying things along, I didn't think it important. He was not a witness, and never spoke... a far cry from his pious intervention yesterday.'

'Though you did say that he'd agreed to perform the burial service at Ebbfield.'

'I did,' Boyd nodded. 'It was much talked about, among those who attended.'

We fell silent as we entered the old village of Kempsey. The church with its tall tower was ever prominent, and here we reined in. The place was quiet, the morning's service done. Having dismounted, we led our mounts to a horse trough and allowed them a drink. A few people paused to look our way, whereupon I hailed the nearest one, an old man, and asked the whereabouts of the parsonage.

'Behind the church, Master,' he replied. 'But you won't find parson there just now. I would try the inn.'

He jerked his thumb towards it, whereupon I gave him thanks... and on a sudden, I thought of Woolland as he had appeared that day in the courtyard at Ebbfield, mounted and clad in hunting attire. It sat poorly with the fiery rhetorician I had heard at the burial, and at yesterday's inquest. As for his being at the inn... well, many a parson is in the habit of quenching his thirst after a sermon, I told myself.

Without further word, the two of us led our horses the short distance, found a post and tethered them. On entering the inn, we paused to look about. The place was almost empty, save for a sweating drawer hefting a barrel on to its cruck. There were few tables and fewer drinkers, and the man we sought was nowhere to be seen. As I scanned the room, the inn's host finished his task and turned to us. Noting our swords and our attire, he grinned at once.

'Welcome, sirs. I pray you, be seated... have you come far?'

'Not far,' I replied as he came closer, wiping his hands on his apron. 'We seek Parson Woolland. Is he not here?'

I too wore a smile, but it faded as the inn-keeper stopped and lowered his gaze. 'I... the matter is, sir... your pardon, but he is not.'

A moment passed, in which neither Boyd nor I spoke. Had the

man known who we were, I thought, perhaps he might have made a better fist of lying, but as it was…

'I think he is,' I said.

The other looked up. 'Nay, sir, I do assure you…'

'You do not assure me. I'm a former Justice of Worcester, who takes a poor view of liars. Do you care to think again?'

The fellow gulped, glanced at Boyd then back at me, busily wiping his hands. 'Now I think on it, he was here,' he said, making a show of looking around. 'Likely he's out the back… if you'll seat yourselves, I'll go and see while someone serves you.'

'Yet, it looks as if there's no-one serving apart from yourself,' Boyd put in, raising his brows. 'Is there no wench here?'

At that, I felt inclined to smile; my friend had gone straight to the nub of the matter, causing our host to falter. Pointedly I looked at the stairway in the corner, then up at the ceiling.

'Perhaps the parson prefers a private room,' I suggested. 'Do you have one?'

'Well… I do, sir,' the inn-keeper admitted. 'But it's-'

'Taken?' I finished. 'No matter. If you've no objection, I'd like to view it anyway.'

The poor man appeared quite miserable now. 'Nay, sir, I pray you… likely the room is bolted, and my guest is engaged upon some private matter…'

He broke off as I laid a hand on his shoulder. 'Yet I mean to go up there,' I said. 'I'm sure you wouldn't wish to hinder a former Justice, engaged in lawful investigation.'

It was not the first time I had been on tenuous legal ground, but it was enough. With a sickly look, the host could only watch as Boyd and I strode past him to the stairs.

There were two doors on the upper floor, beneath the sloping roof. The first stood open, so I walked to the other one and knocked, the doctor close behind me. Almost at once, we heard muffled sounds from within. I tried the door, but as the inn-keeper had said, it was bolted.

'Open!' I called out, rattling the latch for good measure. 'I have business with Thomas Woolland.'

For a while nothing happened, though when I pressed my ear

to the planking I believed I heard voices. I knocked again, more loudly, and was at last rewarded by a scraping of the bolt. Whereupon, as soon as I adjudged it free, I pushed the door open with some force, stepped inside the room with hand on sword… and froze.

Parson Woolland, tousle-haired, bare-legged and clad in only a shirt, was backing away from me. While behind him…

Behind him, cowering on a low bed in the corner and hiding her nakedness with a sheet, was a pale, red-haired girl no older than eleven or twelve years.

Nobody said a word. Keeping my eyes on Woolland, I moved further into the room, causing him to retreat until he was backed up against the wall. Meanwhile Boyd stepped in, assessed the situation quickly and looked to the bed.

'Are you here of your own will, my girl?' He asked kindly.

Plainly terrified, the young maid nodded.

'You were not coerced in any way?' He persisted. 'We mean you no harm, so speak.'

'All is well, sir – I swear it,' she blurted.

'Then, perhaps it's best you took your clothes and left us,' the doctor said. 'Will that serve?'

Nodding vigorously, the girl hurried to comply. Wrapping the sheet about herself, she scrambled from the bed and moved to a stool where her clothing was piled. Seizing it in a bundle, bare-footed and somewhat shaky, she swerved past Boyd and fled from the room. To the sound of her feet pattering along the passage, we turned our attention upon Woolland.

'Well now,' I said. 'We're all sinners, sir… but some sins are more grievous than others. Would you not agree?'

The man made no answer. There was no hiding his guilt, and Boyd and I were witnesses to it. How many others, I wondered briefly, had knowledge of their parson's proclivities?

'Were it anyone else, I might ask pardon for disturbing him at such a time,' I went on, feeling my anger rising. 'Yet, given the age of the other party-'

'I pray you, let me alone!' Woolland cried, finding his voice at last.

'I will not,' I said. 'I came here to ask questions of you, but

89

now…' I glanced at Boyd. 'The case is altered, isn't it?'

'I would say it is,' Boyd said. And at the look in his eye, the parson faltered.

'I have done no crime,' he muttered.

'I doubt if that's how an archdeaconry court would view it,' I told him. 'More, I wonder how your parishioners would?'

That shook the man. Until now, despite being caught as he had, I had been uncertain whether Woolland would try to bluff, or even fall back on some pious rant. Now, I confess I was enjoying the fact that he was at my mercy - an opportunity not to be missed.

'Do they know what you get up to?' I enquired. 'I would think it hard to keep secrets, in a place like this. And given the eagerness many village folk have for denouncing their neighbours – even a man of God.'

'Unless he has protection of some kind,' Boyd said, on a sudden. I stiffened; a notion was forming. I caught his glance, then faced Woolland again.

'Let me ask you this,' I said, fixing him with my magistrate's eye. 'Since you stated plainly at the inquest yesterday that you would not bury a suicide, then why were you willing to conduct the funeral of Susanna Cobbett?'

Rapidly he sought for an answer, his eyes moving between the doctor and I. 'The burial was on Cobbett land, not the church's,' he said. 'I pitied him in his loss and his plight – I did but help a neighbour in his hour of need.'

'No… that won't serve.'

I took another step forward, making him flinch. 'You speak to one who's dealt with some of the best liars in the county. And I know Giles Cobbett's a powerful man, the richest landowner for miles – but tell me, Master Woolland, what kind of hold does he have over you?'

And when he failed to answer, I raised my hand and pointed a finger to within an inch of his chest. 'Speak,' I ordered. 'Or I'll draw my own conclusions, haul you off to Worcester by force and swear out a warrant. I'm unsure what the charge will be, but I'll make sure everyone in the city knows of your arrest – and half the shire, too. Whatever the consequences, you're finished. Bishop Thornborough's a stern man – but you won't need me to tell you that.'

Tense as a bowstring, Woolland gazed at the floor. From below, familiar inn sounds drifted: voices, the clink of tankards. The parson opened his mouth, closed it again - then all at once he sagged, and I tasted victory. A scrawny figure, with his dirty toes and spindly legs, he folded to the floor like an empty sack and fell back against the wall, hugging his shirt about him.

'God in heaven, forgive me,' he whispered hoarsely.

Whereupon he looked up, fixed me with a baleful look, and spoke in what I can only describe as a snarl.

'What a meddler you are, Belstrang,' he spat. 'A wastrel and a varlet at heart... one who lives in fornication with a servant, yet dares to judge me!' And seeing my anger rise, he gave a bitter laugh.

'Must I spell it out?' He cried. 'I buried the Cobbett girl at Ebbfield because she was a scarlet whore, a Jezebel unfit to walk hallowed earth, and because-'

'You're lying!'

Raising a fist, I could have struck the man, had not Boyd hurried to stay me. Breathing hard, I allowed him to push my arm down, and took a step back. But despite my anger, I was triumphant: the truth was plain.

'That's not the reason,' I said. 'You did it because Cobbett forced you – because he threatened to expose you for the foul, child-using devil you are. You laid his daughter to rest because you had no choice - will you deny it?'

He could not. With an effort I mastered myself, Boyd and I standing over the wretched Woolland. The sorriest rogue I ever knew: a pious zealot, quick to call down the wrath of God on everyone but himself.

With a muttered oath, I turned from him and made for the door.

FOURTEEN

It was Boyd who questioned Parson Woolland further, after I had gone down the stairs. I did not see the inn-keeper; in truth I looked neither to left nor right as I went. Outside, I stood beside Leucippus for a while, breathing in sweet air with a scent of mown grass. Presently the doctor emerged, and without a word we got ourselves mounted. Not until we had put Kempsey behind us, and were well on the road, did I ask him what had occurred.

'It's most odd,' he answered. 'That one's a sorry excuse for a parson, but he's also a frightened man beneath his bluster - and not merely because he fears his sins being found out.'

I took in his words, and waited.

'He was loth to speak to me, of course, but I sensed something,' he went on. 'Were he a Papist I'd describe him as being eager to make Confession, and to do some sort of penance. As it is, I think he's desperate to unburden himself to someone.'

'Well he might be,' I muttered.

'Indeed, and yet...' Boyd frowned. 'You hit the nail aright, when you accused him of being under Cobbett's thumb. But instead, I thought to press him further in the matter of your friend Mistress Mason - and the accusations against her.'

I turned sharply to him. 'What did he say?'

'Only what you would expect: that she was a demon in female form who must be destroyed, and so forth. I left him soon after, being mighty tired of his company.' He paused, then: 'Yet there is a puzzlement here, Robert... this unholy and strange-looking link between Woolland, Cobbett and-'

'And his tenant, Humphreys,' I finished. In truth, I had thought the same: that private smile I had seen exchanged at the graveside, and could not forget.

'Do you have any tasks this afternoon?' I asked, on impulse.

'Nothing pressing...' The doctor eyed me warily. 'What action are you proposing now?'

'None, for the present. I was intending to invite you to ride home with me, take dinner at Thirldon and then help me tease this business out. I would welcome your insight. Will you honour me?'

'Will we dine alone, or with Mistress Hester?' Boyd enquired. 'For I generally value her insight too… don't you?'

I threw him a rueful look, and eased Leucippus to a faster gait as the spires of Worcester came into view.

***

After dinner, we sat outdoors at my garden table in the company of a jug of wine, as well as in the company of Hester. And, since there was no gainsaying him, that of Childers too. I had already given them an account of what had transpired in Kempsey, which distressed Hester a good deal. Having voiced her opinion, that Woolland was unfit to be in holy orders, she had fallen silent on the matter. Now, with all said and done, we assembled like a council of war – or rather like a jury mulling over the evidence, before realising that there was precious little of it.

'I've turned it over until I'm giddy,' I admitted. 'I thought to uncover a design to have Agnes Mason hanged, so that Cobbett could seize her bit of land, whether he thinks there's gold buried there or not. Now, it feels murkier… as if some conspiracy lies beneath, the purpose of which eludes me.'

'It eludes me too,' Boyd murmured. 'Yet I'll allow that conspiracies sometimes exist. Will we ever forget the Powder Treason, and what might have been had it succeeded?'

I glanced at Hester: neither of us wished to revisit that topic, given my involvement in uncovering the Anniversary Plot, which to most people's knowledge never existed.

'Yet as matters stand, sir, you must concede that Giles Cobbett has what he wants,' Childers said, having waited to make his contribution with impatience. 'Both of those young people now adjudged suicides, and believed by everyone to have been driven to madness by witchery. When those facts are put before a jury-'

'I'm well aware of it,' I broke in, with my withering look. 'And moreover…' I glanced at Boyd. 'It looks if all those in

93

Cobbett's circle – for a circle it appears to me – are prepared to hide the truth, or even lie under oath, to further him in his aims.' I was thinking of the testimony of William Mount, who claimed to have found the body, and of the Powick constable, but especially that of Eliza Dowling.

'Or in the case of Justice Standish, to dispute evidence that doesn't suit him,' Boyd said. 'Or to refuse to hear it.'

'Hence, you stand alone,' Hester put in, looking at me. With the eyes of all three of us upon her, she added: 'Standish is the Magistrate, who will have conference with the judge at Quarter Sessions. Hence, who remains to listen to your theories? Provided you have any, that is.'

None of us spoke, until Childers chose to break the silence.

'Some might say that you have done all you can for that woman, sir,' he ventured.

I met his eye, and saw only concern for me; to him, the matter was all but closed. Yet he had not seen Agnes Mason in her cell, nor the distress of her son and daughter-in-law… I took a drink, but made no reply.

And indeed, it seemed there was little more to be said; as a council of war the afternoon was a failure. To go against Giles Cobbett, and those who stood ready to support him, now seemed fruitless. What, indeed, was my cause? As for theories, as Hester had said, I had none to speak of: only unease over Susanna Cobbett's death, suspicion of murder done to Howell Rhys, and a smouldering anger that an innocent woman was to be sent to the gallows.

Hence, after some further desultory talk we rose from the table, Hester to deal with household matters and Boyd to go to his duties in Worcester. I walked with him to the stables, and once we were alone, begged a small service from him: I asked him to visit the Guildhall and enquire as to the condition of Agnes Mason.

'Her condition?' He raised his eyebrows.

'The jailer, Burton, is a varlet,' I told him. 'He may tamper with her food. But if Sergeant Lisle is there, you may ask him on my behalf.'

He hesitated, then: 'You have taken that woman's welfare to

heart, have you not?'

'It's what I would do for any prisoner whom I think has been wrongly accused,' I answered, to which he gave a sigh, and signalled his consent.

After seeing him ride away I stood in the stable yard, absently watching Elkins leading one of the mares out for exercise. The afternoon was already waning, and having a mind to be alone I intended to go to my private parlour to read.But it was then, as I turned away, that Elkins halted by the gateway and called out. I looked round, hearing a sound of hooves approaching, and saw a lone horseman enter the yard. He slowed his mount, then drew rein and looked directly at me.

'Would you be Master Belstrang, sir? Justice Belstrang?'

'I would.' I looked him over, seeing a grey-haired, ruddy-faced man in plain garb, mounted on an old sway-backed horse. 'And who might you be?'

'David ap Rhys, sir... I've ridden from Powick. I got there too late for the inquest yesterday, but I know what passed.' He let out a sigh. 'Might I speak with you?'

'Of course - I pray you, dismount.'

I called to Elkins to see to the visitor's horse. And soon David ap Rhys, whose border accent I had now recognised, stood before me. He was the father of Howell Rhys, he explained, though I already knew.

'You look weary, Master Rhys,' I said. 'Will you come in and take some refreshment?'

'Most gladly, sir.' He paused, then: 'Yet before all else, I desire to thank you most heartily – you and the other gentleman, the doctor, for standing up for my son as you did.'

'I think the doctor may have earned your thanks,' I said, taken aback. 'I did little.'

Rhys shook his head firmly. 'Nay, sir - you refused to condemn my boy, as others have done. And I will say more, if you'll hear me.'

'Well now, I will indeed,' I said.

***

It was a sad tale, told by a man ragged with grief. He sat at the well-scrubbed table in the Thirldon kitchen, having eaten a little food and now clutching a mug of beer. He talked with pride of Howell, the youngest of his three sons. The boy had been a fine shepherd, but was not needed so much on their farm now that his brothers were working it. He had been content to go and work for Rowden, not meaning to stay more than two years. But then he had encountered Mistress Cobbett when she was out riding, and everything changed.

'He did love her most fiercely, Master Belstrang,' Rhys told me. 'He sent me letters... I don't read too well, but my eldest boy does. Howell had plans... he was going to get the maid away from her father, which she too desired, being most unhappy. He wouldn't leave the county without her - he swore it.'

Recalling Jane Cobbett's testimony that morning by the crossing, I nodded. 'From what I know, his sentiments were returned,' I said. 'Did he speak of swimming the river by night, to keep tryst with her?'

'He did,' Rhys said at once. 'He was always a fine swimmer, and unafraid. Indeed, his courage was well known...' he broke off suddenly, fixing me with a keen eye.

'Which is why I say to you now, sir, that my son would never have taken his own life. I know it, as all of us who were his kinfolk know it. And whatever befell that poor maid, he would have toiled to find out what lay behind it – for I know in my heart there's more to that than has been told!'

'And by heaven, so do I,' I answered, after a moment. 'In truth, I've thought so from the start. Nor do I believe your son was bewitched and made mad – any more than Susanna Cobbett was.'

The other drew a long breath. 'It warms my heart to hear you say so. But then...' a haggard look appeared. 'It can mean only one thing, Master Belstrang: that he was murdered.'

I made no reply; though I too believed that, I was uneasy about voicing it. For a while Rhys seemed lost in thought, gazing down at the table. Finally, he looked up.

'Do you have any notion as to who would do that? And why?' He asked, speaking softly.

I hesitated. 'If I did, I would be slow to name them,' I

answered finally. For there was a spark in the man's eye now: an urge, naturally enough, to settle the score, which discomfited me. Justice, not vengeance, was my watchword. I decided not to speak of what Jane Cobbett told me, of how her father threatened Howell Rhys's life – but the next moment, I was confounded.

'Yet I would not,' David ap Rhys said. 'I will name the father of the girl Howell loved... the same man who forbade him to see her.' His voice rose as he spoke, until it was filled with anger. 'A cold-hearted man who kept his daughters penned up like cattle, yet might have burned to avenge the one who died-'

'I pray you - no more, Master Rhys.'

I cut him short, shaking my head. To suspect Giles Cobbett of such a crime was one thing, but to act upon that suspicion was something quite different.

'There's no proof,' I told him. 'Even my friend Doctor Boyd, who spoke at the inquest, would tell you the same. The man you accuse is wealthy and powerful. To gather enough evidence to bring such a charge against him would be...' I hesitated. 'It would be all but impossible.'

After that we were silent for a while. The kitchen was deserted, since I'd told everyone to leave me alone with the visitor. Indicating the jug of beer, I invited Rhys to take a refill, but he shook his head.

'I must ride back to Powick before nightfall. I have a bed with some folk who took pity on me – which is more than most have done. The constable, he would barely tell me anything. And as for that parson...' he looked away briefly. 'I've heard enough about him. But to the devil with the fellow... I'll be taking my son home tomorrow, to let him lie at peace among those who knew him and loved him.'

I barely nodded; I was saddened, even ashamed. Had I truly advised him to let the matter drop, I thought, knowing that his son had likely been murdered? Could I have done the same, had the victim been my daughter? I sought for some words of comfort, but found none.

After a moment, Rhys got to his feet. 'I thank you for your kindness, Master Belstrang,' he said in a tired voice. 'Now it's best that I be on my way.'

I too arose, feeling the man's grief as I saw how it weighed upon him… whereupon:

'Wait,' I said, after drawing a breath.

He turned to face me.

'Ten days ago,' I told him, 'a man called Mason came to me for help, which I have tried to deliver. In truth, I've made small progress since - at times, it almost feels as if I've gone backwards. But let me say this to you, Master Rhys: I make no promises, but I swear I'll not let the matter rest. Not until I've done all I can to bring about justice – and yes, perhaps retribution. If I can discover what happened to your son, I will do it. So, when you take Howell back to the Welsh Borders tomorrow, will you go in the knowledge that I wish to see this through to the end? Can you do that, for my sake if no other?'

Rhys regarded me without expression. I even wondered if he hesitated to trust me… until a smile formed.

'I will go with a lighter heart than I thought possible, but an hour ago,' he said. 'And even if you fail, it will be of comfort to me to know that someone here cared enough to try.'

Whereupon we walked out through the doors together, shook hands and parted. A few minutes later I watched the father of Howell Rhys ride away on his old sway-backed horse. He neither waved nor looked back, but I fancied he sat a little more erect in the saddle.

But my moment of satisfaction was of short duration. The following morning, I learned that Ned Berritt had been found dead.

FIFTEEN

I received the news at mid-day, when a courier arrived bearing a message from Boyd. It seemed Berritt had been found not at one of usual haunts, but floating in the Severn near Tait's Crossing. Normally a body would be carried downriver by the current, but it had been caught up in reeds on the eastern bank, where Dan Tait himself had found it. He had sent word to Worcester, whence the matter had been passed to the acting Coroner: one Justice Standish.

Within the hour I was in the city once again, conferring with the doctor.

'It's preposterous,' I told him. 'A man like Berritt would never have drowned – he knew every inch of the water.'

Boyd was silent, sitting in his chair, eyes lowered.

'And more,' I went on, 'I'll wager his body had been there for two days at the least – which is why he never appeared at the inquest. Do you see?'

I spoke with some heat, as theories had been buffeting my mind for the past hour. Since my speech with David ap Rhys the day before, I took the matter personally. Pacing the room, my hat in my hand, I was about to say more when Boyd looked up.

'What should I see, Robert?' He enquired.

'That the man was murdered. Will you doubt it?'

'I might, since I've not seen the evidence,' he replied after a moment. 'Though I'll agree that it looks suspicious. Yet before you ask, I won't be allowed to examine the body. Our friend Standish has already ruled that out.'

'How so?' I demanded.

'Because, in view of your close interest in the recent deaths, I took the trouble to go to his house directly after hearing the news and suggested it. He was too busy to receive me, but sent his servant to inform me that another physician would be appointed. I know not who it is.'

'But that smacks of corruption,' I exclaimed. 'Berritt was a

99

vital witness in the matter of Rhys's death, who would have cast doubt on other testimonies – now he's dead. I know it was by design, as I believe I know who had reason to silence him-'

'Robert, stay yourself.' Boyd was frowning. 'Are we to tread this ground again? If you mean to accuse Giles Cobbett, you will merely add to your troubles. For even if...' he paused, then: 'Even if the man had reason to silence Berritt, and was prepared to go to such desperate lengths, do you not think he would take steps to ensure he could never be linked to the crime? He has the means to buy whomever he chooses – even murderers.'

'And constables and parsons too, it seems,' I said, with some bitterness. 'Well, we spoke yesterday of conspiracies. Will you now agree that this looks mightily like one?'

'Perhaps,' he admitted. 'But to what end?'

'To have the deaths of both Susanna Cobbett and her swain declared self-murder, by virtue of being made mad by Agnes Mason, thereby making her conviction all but certain.'

'And then?'

'And then he can seize her land, for whatever purpose...'

I broke off, a frown coming on. On a sudden, I felt a pang of doubt. I recalled Agnes's words, in her cell at the Guildhall: *the land's good for little but pasture...* I eyed Boyd, who wore his sceptical look.

'When all's considered, what purpose do you think he has?' He asked. 'This fairy-tale of buried gold? He's a wealthy man – he even allows a tenant to fall behind with the rent. Why then, do you think he would go to so much trouble to remove one who does pay it?'

'And more,' Boyd continued, seeing I had no answer, 'if you believe Cobbett's behind the death of Rhys, and now Berritt, why did he not simply arrange an accident for Mason – or even hire an assassin to cut her throat and throw her in the river?'

Feeling somewhat spent, I sank down on a chair – but on a sudden, I knew what I would do next.

'I mean to go downriver now,' I said. 'I'll find Dan Tait, and wring every scrap of intelligence out of the old rogue. For if Berritt was murdered there would be signs on his body – and I'm not about to listen to any more lies, from anyone.'

With that, I stood up to leave – and before my friend could speak, I shook my head.

'No... I thank you for the offer you're going to make, but on this occasion, I think it best I go alone.'

***

An urgency was upon me now, though in truth I knew not why. I ate no dinner, but rode out of Worcester by Frog Gate and took the Tewkesbury Road once again. Having covered the distance in a short time I reached the crossing, where Dan Tait's boat was moored to the bank. There was no sign of the ferryman. I dismounted, tethered Leucippus and walked to the riverside.

All was calm. A breeze rippled the water's surface, while nearby a heron rose at my approach, soaring off to the far bank. In the distance I could see the tree-tops of Newland Wood, favoured haunt of the man who had once stood before me in the dock, and later taken revenge by shooting an arrow so close, I had feared for my life. I saw him yet, with his bow on his shoulder, amused by my discomfort. Deep in thought as I was, I was startled when a voice hailed me.

'You want to cross, sir? If you do, I can't take the horse.'

I turned quickly to see the figure of Dan Tait in a greasy jerkin, his face all but covered by his thick beard. As always, he wore a wide-brimmed hat pulled so low, his eyes could barely be seen. He had appeared from behind a tree, and was still lacing his breeches.

'You should a' hailed me, sir,' he said, coming forward. 'Scared me proper you did, galloping up like that.'

'I wasn't galloping, Master Tait,' I said. 'And nor do I wish to cross the river, so you needn't fret about my horse.'

'So, how can I aid you?' Planting his feet firmly on the ground, the ferryman regarded me with suspicion.

'Do you not remember me?' I asked. 'You stood before me once, accused of affray. You got off, as I recall.'

'By the Christ... Justice Belstrang.' As recognition dawned, Tait grew taut. 'Well now, the day is full of surprises,' he said sourly. 'What do you want with me?'

'I'd like to talk to you about the finding of Ned Berrit's body,'

I said, taking a few steps towards him.

'And what makes you think I'll talk to you?' The other answered. 'You're not a Justice now, and we're not in court.'

'No, we're not,' I agreed. 'And hence, I'm not constrained by any legal niceties.' I placed my hand on my sword and did my best to look threatening.

'Is that so?' Tait scowled. 'You seem a mite bad-tempered today, sir. The matter is, I'm somewhat busy, so-'

'You found Berritt,' I broke in.

'What if I did?' Came the retort.

'I want to know how the body appeared. For you know as well as I do that he didn't drown – he'd fished this river from boyhood. So, tell me.'

'How it appeared?' Tait made a show of pondering. 'Wet, is how I'd put it. Wet, and bedraggled as a water-rat...' but seeing my rising impatience, he trailed off. And when I made as if to draw my sword, he flinched.

'Listen, it wasn't me saw him first,' he said. 'I brought some folk across the water... one of them pointed the body out, tangled in reeds. I told them I'd deal with it, which I did. Hauled it out, then sent word. And that's the end of it.'

'I don't think it is,' I said, stepping closer to him. 'You hauled the body out, you say - was that after your customers had gone?' And when he merely nodded: 'So you saw Berritt at close quarters. What were his injuries?'

'Injuries?' Tait shook his head quickly. 'I saw none. I'd no desire to look close at him. Likely he was drunk and fell in, somewhere upriver-'

'You lying rogue.'

Now I did draw my sword - somewhat clumsily I admit, but it served its purpose. Levelling it at Tait's throat, I leaned forward. 'You know he would never be so careless,' I said. 'And I think you know how he died, so speak!'

A moment passed, in which Tait looked down at my sword, still scowling. 'You've no call for that,' he said harshly.

'I'm waiting,' I told him. 'But let me help you. Was there blood on his clothing? Or perhaps his neck was broken. I pray you, try and remember.'

And yet, nervous though he was, the man remained defiant. 'I saw no blood,' he snapped. 'He'd been in the river for hours… if the water wasn't low just now, he'd have been carried away. And how would I know if his neck was broke? I'm no surgeon.'

I paused, allowing my gaze to stray to the river's bank where his boat was tied… and a notion sprang up.

'Well, mayhap he did drown.' Fixing my eyes on Tait's, I watched him closely. 'If he'd been knocked senseless first, perhaps, then his hands and feet bound tightly… someone would only need to throw him in, wouldn't they?'

He gave no reply, but a look flickered across his features; it vanished at once, but I had seen enough. 'In which case, all you had to do was untie him, get rid of the rope and report a drowning,' I went on. 'Hence, what I want to know, Master Tait, is who paid you? Could it be Giles Cobbett?'

'See now… don't ask me more, Master Belstrang.' On a sudden, Tait lowered his gaze. 'I'm just a waterman… I do my work and stay out of trouble.'

'Well, it seems you've failed in that,' I told him. 'I could swear out a warrant accusing you of aiding a murder – or even conspiracy to murder. How would that be?'

'You wouldn't…' he swallowed, as the words sank in. 'See now, I'm a poor man. I can't afford enemies…'

'That's true enough. But I may think again, if you tell me all you know.' I drew a breath. 'And I swear, I'm not leaving here until you do.'

'Sweet Jesus.' In agitation, Tait shifted on his feet. 'What if I did tell you things? Not that I'm saying I could, only-'

'I'll try and keep your name out of it,' I said. 'Though I can't promise, in such a grave matter as murder.'

'Listen, I know nothing about any murder!' He cried. 'And in God's name, will you lower your blade? I'm like to shit my breeches!'

I lowered it, but only as far as his stomach. 'Spill your tale,' I ordered.

He swallowed, let out a breath, and spoke rapidly.

'I told you, I'm but a waterman. Someone comes to me, asks me to do him a service now and then, and pays me well, how can I refuse him? Given he's a man you don't say no to, I mean. And if he tells me there might be a body showing up, what should I do but drag it from the shallows and report a drowning? It's not unknown, hereabouts...'

'Was he trussed up?' I demanded, cutting him short. 'And if so, did you untie him?'

He made no answer.

'This someone, who asks you to do him a service now and then,' I persisted. 'If his name was Giles Cobbett, whose land lies within mere walking distance from here, might I take your silence for an admission?'

Tait did stay silent. Yet my relief at having drawn this from him was at once tinged with unease: this was becoming most serious. How should I deal with the intelligence I now possessed? I took a step back from the rogue and lowered my sword's tip to the ground... whereupon a notion flew up that made me start. Tait saw it, and shied away by instinct.

'By the Christ, are you not done with me?' He demanded.

'Hear me out first,' I said. 'Two weeks ago, Giles Cobbett's daughter Susanna was found dead at the Witching Pool, over there in Newland.' I pointed across the river. 'It's common knowledge, and you'll know it as most people do. What most people don't know is that men – two of them at least - were in the vicinity of the pool that same night. They had no horses, so I think someone took them across the river. Who else knows the water as well as you, and could ferry them over in the dark? Might that be another of the small services your paymaster asked of you, Master Tait? I would like an answer.'

With that I waited, until at last the old rogue sagged.

'See now - I never took 'em across,' He stated, with a muttered oath. 'I loaned them the boat, it's true, but I didn't go. My eyes aren't so good as they were... besides, they didn't want me. Said they could find their way and bring the boat back, and all I need do was keep quiet. That's the truth - I swear it!'

Determined as he was to free himself of blame, I believed him... but there was more. I felt it, even as I saw the beads of sweat that ran down his cheek. It was a warm day, but...

'Two men,' I said. 'And you knew them.'

Morosely, Tait looked at the ground. 'It was dark… I couldn't swear to it,' he muttered.

'I seem to recall there was a moon that night,' I said. 'But no matter. Let me guess: they were in the service of the same man I've already named. One of them might have been a certain William Mount - do I hit the mark?'

At that Tait looked up sharply. 'No,' he said. 'And Mount doesn't serve Cobbett now…'

'But he used to,' I finished, with some satisfaction: at last, the question of who had ordered Mount to turn me away from the Witching Pool, and then to give false testimony at the inquest into Howell Rhys's death, was cleared up. 'So – who were the two who borrowed your boat?'

He would not answer, merely repeating that it had been dark.

'That won't do,' I said, growing impatient again. 'I need to know who they were. I repeat: it could be a capital crime we speak of. I said I'll try to spare your name, but-'

'Damn you, do you mean to send me to my grave?'

Wild-eyed, Tait stared at me. 'Do you not think he would know who told you?' He cried. 'And do you not think he'd carry out his threat, to have me slain? He doesn't bluff… he'd squash me like a gnat! I'll not name him, and you can go to hell!'

But he was too late. I had fallen into my magistrate's ways, and teased out what I needed: that one of the men who had taken his boat and crossed the river that night, was no less a personage than Giles Cobbett himself.

I sheathed my sword and glanced at Leucippus, who was cropping grass peacefully. 'I won't ask who the other man was,' I said. 'For it scarcely matters.'

Tait threw me a baleful look; but I was already on my way, with renewed purpose.

SIXTEEN

At Thirldon that evening I called Childers to my private chamber after supper, and told him all that I had learned. I knew it would dismay him, but the time was passed for indecision. I would write a letter, I told him, containing a full account of my discoveries. In the event of anything happening to me, this was to be copied and sent to men of rank: Sir Samuel Sandys, the High Sheriff of Worcester, and Sir Edward Coke, the Chief Justice in London - even to Justice Standish. I was about to say more, but seeing the look on my steward's face, I invited him to speak.

'This sounds so doleful, sir. What do you fear might happen to you? Or should I ask, what is it you propose to do?'

I did not answer immediately. Since leaving Dan Tait at the riverside, I had turned the matter over to the exclusion of all else, only to end up dissatisfied. For as yet, I had no firm evidence to accuse Giles Cobbett of anything, though in my heart I felt sure he was involved in the deaths of both Howell Rhys and Ned Berritt, at the least. A man like Dan Tait was not a good witness, and might even change his story. I thought briefly of others, like Humphreys, who would always defend Cobbett. I thought of Agnes Mason, awaiting likely execution – and finally I thought of the one whose death had begun this whole chain of events: Susanna Cobbett, whose own father had crossed the river with another man on that fateful night. Beyond that I had only vague suspicions, but I arrived at one conclusion: I saw no other course than to go to Ebbfield again, confront Cobbett and demand he respond to my questions, or face the consequences.

I drew a breath and told Childers. I expected an outburst, but he surprised me.

'You will not go there alone.'

It was not a question. I met his gaze, my impulse being to reprimand him. But his concern was clearly for me above all else; then, when had it not been?

'I suppose not,' I said finally. 'I should take witnesses-'

'Like me,' Childers broke in. 'And an escort – a small one, perhaps, but made up of stout Thirldon men.'

'I had thought to ask Doctor Boyd to accompany me,' I said, still taken aback. 'But I hesitate to involve him in-'

'Anything that might turn unpleasant?' Childers suggested. 'That would seem wise.'

'I confess to surprise, if not amazement, at your change of heart,' I said, to which he let out a sigh.

'You have often let your own heart rule your head, sir... I saw it from when you were a youth. And since justice is your spur, what can I do but serve you?'

He fell silent, until I gave way to a smile. 'You don't think we're both somewhat old for such an escapade, then?'

'Likely we are,' he replied. 'But age doesn't seem to stop you from bustling about the shire, getting embroiled in other people's troubles. And I can still wear a sword as well as you. Have you forgotten how your father arranged for me to have the rank of gentleman?'

'I have not.'

'So, when do you intend to set out for Ebbfield?'

'In the morning about nine of the clock,' I answered. 'And I pray you, say nothing to Mistress Hester.'

***

The sun was already warm, it being one of those days in May which heralds the coming summer. My party rode at a steady pace into Worcester, then out again on to the Tewkesbury road. It consisted of Childers and myself, my groom Elkins, my manservant Lockyer who had once been a soldier, and the two gardeners, the stoutest men at Thirldon. Six of us in all: enough to furnish an escort, yet not enough to appear a threat. Apart from Childers and I, the others knew little of my intent save that I required protection, which was enough. It gave me a measure of pride to have them at my back.

Nothing was said as we approached Ebbfield and crossed the moat. At the gatehouse I slowed Leucippus to a walk, the other men doing the same. But when we passed under the arch, we found activity in the courtyard. There were people about, and someone busy saddling a horse, but this was no hunting party as on the last occasion I was here. It looked more like a scene of disarray, with raised voices, mainly those of women. As we drew rein, Childers at my side, everyone turned to look at us, and a familiar figure hastened forward: the ageing servant I had encountered on the day of the funeral, whose name I now recalled was Matthew.

'Justice Belstrang, sir...' he made a hurried bow. 'Are you come to help us? For God knows, we are sorely in need of it.'

In surprise, I gazed down at him. 'Why, what has occurred?'

In agitation, his hands clasped together, the old man spoke rapidly. 'The girls, sir – they are gone. Did you not know?' Seeing I did not, he added: 'Mistress Jane and Mistress Alison... their beds were found empty this morning. My master has ridden out already, taking every man he could. Even the youngest stable-boy is about to go.' He blinked, gazing up at me. 'I thought you were here to join the search.'

His face was drawn with worry - and I was at once confounded, my purpose dashed. I glanced at Childers, who looked dismayed. What was to be done now?

'Has anyone an inkling as to why they left?' I asked. An image came to mind of Jane Cobbett sitting her horse, her anxious face... it was a week ago.

'It seems not, sir.' Mournfully, Matthew shook his head. 'Though Mistress Dowling might.' I followed his gaze, to see the nurse standing among the handful of servants. I knew she had seen me, though she kept her distance.

'We must help, sir,' Childers said. 'Those girls might be in danger. The more riders there are to scour the country the better, don't you think?'

I could only consent. The other Thirldon men had eased their mounts forward, awaiting instruction. 'Yet, if Cobbett and his men are already abroad, we need some direction,' I said. 'Or we'll all end up chasing our own tails.'

I dismounted, and handed Leucippus' reins to Lockyer. 'I'll speak with Mistress Dowling,' I told Matthew.

'As you wish, sir.'

The old man moved aside. Leaving my companions, I walked

across the cobbles. Servants, maids and kitchen wenches moved away as I approached the nurse. There was no performance from her this time, as at the inquest: she looked taut, even nervous.

'Have you any notion of where they might go, Mistress?' I asked, without preamble.

She hesitated, then: 'I have not, sir.'

'Truly?' I fixed my eyes upon hers. 'You, who know your charges better than anyone?'

She shook her head. 'A prank, perhaps, or a silly game…'

'Somehow I doubt that,' I broke in.

'Well…' she drew herself to full height. 'Whatever the case, we achieve nothing by standing here,' she said frostily. 'I'm no great horsewoman, or I would go out myself. Whereas you and your guards…' her face grew hard. 'For that is how you appear,' she added. 'I would wonder at your purpose, had I not more pressing concerns just now.'

'Then I won't detain you further,' I said, reining in my displeasure at her insolence. 'And should your master return before I do, I pray you tell him that I came to his aid, as I would that of any neighbour in difficulty.'

I turned away – but almost at once, felt a tug on my sleeve.

'Master Belstrang…'

I looked round sharply, and was struck by the sudden change in her manner. There was more than anxiety in her expression: to my surprise, there was fear.

'He… I know my master would thank you,' she said, avoiding my gaze. 'We want nothing other than the safe return of his daughters, as quickly as can be.'

I waited for her to meet my eye; but when she would not, I gave a brief nod and walked back to my party.

The search lasted the entire day, yet brought no result.

At first, after conferring briefly, we had split up and ridden off in pairs: Childers and myself, Elkins with one of the gardeners, Lockyer with the other. Elkins would go east as far as Norton, Lockyer southwards to Kempsey and beyond, as far as Clevelode. It seemed unlikely that two girls without horses could have got any further. And since it appeared that they had gone during the night, they would have moved slowly. I ordered my people to ride every path, search every copse and hedgerow, every barn and byre, calling at farms along the way. Meanwhile Childers and I would backtrack along the Worcester road, skirting the river bank. If the girls were found they should be taken to Ebbfield, riding double with their finders. To which order, it was Lockyer who had raised a troublesome question.

'Supposing they don't want to go home, sir?'

In truth, the thought had already occurred to me. It seemed certain that Cobbett's daughters had run away, in which case…

'Bring them to Tait's Crossing and wait for me,' I said. 'We should all meet there, before sunset.'

Whereupon we had parted, though without much hope on my part. I had a notion Jane Cobbett would have expected a search, and taken steps to thwart it.

Thereafter, the day wore on as Childers and I rode up and down, seeking any trace of the missing girls. We stopped at cottages, questioned travellers and drovers, without success. Twice we encountered Cobbett's mounted servants on the same mission. I spoke to one of them, though his manner was brusque, and he would only say that they had found no sign.

It had occurred to me that Jane might have money, and might have intended to get to Worcester where she could hire a coach. I mentioned it to Childers, who had grown thoughtful throughout the afternoon. When we stopped to drink from our costrels and allow the horses some rest, he spoke up.

'I fear we are wasting our efforts, sir. If those girls have fled their home, for whatever reason, then they would be most careful to avoid discovery. They could even be in hiding, awaiting nightfall.'

'It's possible,' I allowed.

We were on the riverbank, just below the bend where the Teme flows into the Severn, with the rooftops of Powick just visible on the far side. I had thought of venturing there, though it seemed an unlikely destination, and doubtless Cobbett would have considered it. We had seen nothing of the man himself, all day.

'Or, might they have crossed the water?'

He was gazing at the river, scanning the far bank. During the day we had encountered men fishing, but they could tell us nothing. As for Dan Tait: we had stopped at the crossing, but though his boat was moored, he was nowhere to be seen.

'They would have needed help,' I said, thinking of my encounter with the ferryman the day before. But I dismissed the notion: Tait would never dare to involve himself with Giles Cobbett's runaway daughters. More likely he would inform on them at once, in hopes of gaining favour from their father.

On a sudden, Childers yawned; it had been a long day, and he was unused to hard riding. I glanced up; the sun was waning, and it looked as if there was nothing more to be done, but to ride back to the crossing and await the rest of my party.

'We'd best go,' I said.

Somewhat low in spirits, we remounted and headed downriver again, walking the tired horses. Tait's crossing was little more than a mile off, and we were there within the quarter hour to find my servants already waiting.

As I expected they were empty-handed, and had found no trace of the runaways.

***

We returned to Thirldon, where I left the men to take supper and spend the rest of the evening as they pleased. Childers and I supped late with Hester, who was astonished at my news. Knowing she would ask my reason for taking a party to Ebbfield in the first place, I was obliged to give her a brief account of all that had occurred. Seeing how tired and dispirited we both were, she passed no comment.

Yet my own thoughts were in disarray: how should I act, given the new circumstances? Though I knew there had to be good reason for Jane Cobbett and her sister to flee their home, I could hardly confront their father at such a time. In this humour, I at last went to my bed. I had a vague notion of riding to Boyd on the morrow to see if, between us, we could come at some solution. Then I recalled that it would be the Sabbath, which afforded me one small relief: I would sleep late, and hang the consequences.

However, the night was far from over.

I awoke in pitch darkness, hearing the door open. I assumed it was Hester, until I made out the figure of Childers in his night-robe, holding a candle. As I sat up, he called out.

'Your pardon, sir, but you had better rise and come down.'

'What in God's name...?' I began, then paused. Through the open window came sounds: hooves, and the clink of harness.

'There's a cart,' Childers said. 'We have visitors.'

I dressed hurriedly, growing aware of voices and footsteps on the stairs; some of the servants were up. When I emerged from my chamber, I found Hester waiting in her russet night-gown. Together we descended, following Childers through the doors and out into the night air. In the courtyard, where lanterns had been lit, stood a covered cart with two horses stamping and blowing in the shafts. A man I did not recognise was holding the nearside horse, speaking low to calm it. As I looked around, Elkins the groom, a cape thrown over his night-shirt, came walking towards me.

'They won't come out, sir,' he said, frowning. 'They ask for you, and no-one else.'

'What do you mean?' I demanded. 'Who won't come out?'

'The girls.' He gestured towards the cart. 'They're afraid... can you assure them they will come to no harm?'

For a moment I failed to understand. But Hester gave a start, and clutched my arm instinctively.

'Girls...?' I gazed at Elkins, who held out a lantern - and as I took it, realisation struck me. I pointed to the man with the horses. 'Who's that?'

'He drove the cart in, sir,' Elkins answered. 'Woke me up... by the time I came out of the stable he was down on the cobbles. He doesn't say much.'

'Does he not?' I said. 'We'll see.'

Holding the lantern aloft, I walked directly to the cart-driver, who turned at my approach. I was on the point of demanding an explanation, but decided it must wait: his passengers were more important. So I walked to the rear of the wagon, lifted the flap... and froze.

Two faces peered out, blinking in the lantern's glow: Jane and Alison Cobbett, huddled together, wrapped in cloaks. At sight of me they started, then:

'Master Belstrang…' Jane gave vent to a sigh, of mingled relief and exhaustion. 'I pray you, give us sanctuary. We ask you to help us – or if need be, we will beg.'

And she broke into tears, whereupon her sister did the same.

SEVENTEEN

There was no question of speaking with the runaway girls that night. They were brought into the house and given a chamber together, the beds hastily prepared. Hester attended them herself, assuring them that they could remain there as long as they liked, taking breakfast in the room if they desired. Meanwhile, she said, the Justice would inform their father they were safe – but at that, Jane had flown into a panic.

'But he must not!' She had cried. 'Not until I explain - will you ask his promise to wait until then?'

It was done. Hester brought the request to me as I returned to bed and I agreed, if with misgivings. Thereafter, Thirldon slept until the sun was up. When I arose it was with some unease, along with much curiosity: why had the Cobbett girls chosen to come to me?

After breakfast I ventured outdoors, to find that the cart was gone. At once, I sought out Elkins.

'The fellow drove off, sir, soon after I went back to bed,' he said. 'By the time I came out he was away. Didn't even water the horses. I did offer him a pallet, but he wouldn't stay.'

'Did he not say anything?' I asked.

'Only that he was hired to make a delivery of goods, and his work was done.'

I sighed, thinking that I must have slept most soundly not to hear the cart rattle away. But then, it was of little importance: what mattered was to speak with my new charges, to whom I appeared to have given sanctuary. It was mid-day before the opportunity arrived - but when at last it did, it would occasion both amazement and dismay.

The first surprise was that, all the time we had been searching for the runaways, they had been in hiding at a house in Worcester. And when I asked who had hidden them, the answer came as a shock: Parson Thomas Woollard.

'We went to him for two reasons,' Jane said, sitting quietly in my private parlour. 'Firstly, because I believed the Kempsey

114

parsonage was the last place my father would look. And secondly, because I knew I could force Woollard to help us.'

I heard her in silence, as did Hester and Childers, who were seated close by. The sisters sat side by side, calmer now and rested, though both looked pale and taut. Alison said not a word, nor had she from the moment of their arrival.

'He fears my father, but he fears the law even more,' Jane went on. 'As he knows I have knowledge enough to lose him his living – perhaps even his freedom.'

She bit her lip, seemingly unwilling to say more. I exchanged looks with Hester; it was only three days since Boyd and I had caught Woolland at the inn, with a girl young enough to be his grand-daughter.

'In truth, I know something of the parson's ways,' I told her, as kindly as I could. 'You need not fear to accuse him.'

'Accuse him?' Jane echoed. 'I did not dare, sir… but then, he could not be sure of my silence. Which is why, when I roused him and told him what I wanted, he made the arrangements.'

'And what were those?'

'To convey us to Worcester before the night was done, in secret. Then, as soon as the gates were open, to take us somewhere in the city where we could wait out the day. After that, to get us here to Thirldon…' the girl sighed. 'It was the only place I could think of – *you* were the only person I could think of, sir, who might offer the sanctuary we need.'

'I'm flattered,' I said. 'And I do offer it. I suppose, since you knew a search would be mounted, you waited until the middle of the night to complete your journey?'

'In truth, we hoped to come here at dusk,' Jane answered. 'But the carter was very late. I thought Woolland had betrayed us… we were mortally afraid, waiting by the road. We knew not whom to trust.'

I glanced at Hester and Childers, who were as attentive as I was. I had a score of questions, but reined in my impatience.

'So, the parson himself took you to Worcester,' Hester said.

Jane nodded. 'On his horse, we two riding together. He borrowed a mule for himself from somewhere, and led us there by dark, our heads covered. But we met no-one, and by early morning we were in the city, where he knew someone who would shelter us for the day and keep it secret.' She threw a glance at her sister, who still made no sound.

'Who is this person?' I demanded. And when she hesitated, I was obliged to be firm. 'See now, I swear you have nothing to fear – not from me, Mistress Hester or John Childers, who have my absolute trust. But if you desire my help, I need you to tell me everything. Can you not do so?'

A moment passed, then: 'She's an old woman, who keeps a certain kind of house,' Jane said, lowering her eyes. 'There are many rooms there. We were given one below the eaves, and a little food, and told not to come out again until fetched.'

I tensed: at last, I had the picture. 'Were you left alone, until it was time to leave?' I asked, somewhat sharply.

She hesitated again, then uttered words that surprised us further. 'You need not trouble to spare my feelings, Master Belstrang, for I know what a bawdy house is. Yet we were not molested. And I was not surprised to see how familiar Parson Woolland was with the place... nor how well he seemed to know the woman whose house it was.'

I looked at Childers, who shook his head, eyes downcast.

'You said you knew enough to threaten the parson,' I said. 'While visiting such places would perhaps ruin him if it were known, I don't see how-'

'They were children!'

It was Alison who spoke, startling everyone, her voice shrill. 'She kept maids - some my age, even younger,' she cried, looking round angrily at the company. 'We saw them, peering round doors when we left. One looked no more than seven or eight years old!'

She turned to her sister, who kept silent, then faced me. 'You speak of Woolland being in fear? Well, so are we both, sir. And if it were in my power, I would kill him myself!'

Whereupon, giving way to a flood of tears, she jumped to her feet and ran from the room, banging the door behind her. I thought Jane would follow, but before she could rise Hester stood up and placed a hand on her shoulder.

'I will go to her,' she said. 'You can help by telling Master

Belstrang all that you know – will you do so?'

The girl gave a nod. With a sigh she watched Hester leave, then turned her sad eyes upon me.

'Ask me what you like, sir,' she said quietly. 'For I fear I've neither the strength nor the will to keep these secrets any longer. But in the matter of Parson Woollard, it is too late to deal him the justice he deserves. He has fled, perhaps to London, perhaps even further. He swore we would never see him again - which is one blessing, at least.'

Whereupon, having taken a drink of weak ale, she at last told her story – which chills me now, as I think on it.

***

Susanna, being the eldest, had been the first to suffer. Even before her mother died, she was the victim of her father's lustful attentions in secret. It had gone on for years, until she was old enough to protest, by which time Jane too knew what went on behind the locked door of her sister's chamber. Yet they were afraid to speak – even to their mother.

'To this day, I do not know how much my mother knew,' Jane said, biting back tears. 'But she became ill, growing weaker by the day until at last she could not leave her bed. Then she died, and all the while my father had his way, growing bolder. Until the day came when he learned of Howell, and his night-time visits.'

She shook her head. 'Father is a cruel man, yet I never saw him so angry as the day he found out. I believe he could have slain Howell.' She sighed. 'And now that he's dead...'

'You think your father killed him?' I broke in, unable to keep the question back.

'I cannot know. He could have got someone else...' on a sudden, her face hardened. 'Abel Humphreys, for one. That varlet... he would have been glad to do it.'

'Will you say more of Humphreys?' I asked. 'For I'm most curious to know-' I stopped, jolted by a new notion. Once again, I pictured Humphreys and Cobbett that day at the graveside. I looked at Childers, who was aghast, then back at Jane. 'Was he also a party to your father's wicked practices?' I asked – to which, her expression was answer enough.

'Not merely landlord and tenant, but brothers in lust.' Jane met my eye, her face taut with bitterness. 'He would cross the river by Tait's boat and come to Ebbfield some nights, to share Susanna as if she were a whore. And he way he looked at me…' She paused, then: 'It was but a matter of time. I never told anyone until now. It feels as if a yoke is being lifted.'

For a while after that I was speechless. It was past dinner-time, yet I had no appetite; nor did Childers. But when I suggested to Jane that we cease our discourse for a while and walk in the gardens, she shook her head. There was an urgency upon her to finish her testimony, now she had begun. Later, she said, she would go to her sister. And hence, what could I do but let her continue?

'She would tell me everything… Susanna, I mean,' Jane said. 'After our mother died, we began to make plans to run away. She knew that, as I was now becoming a woman too, father would turn his attentions to me – and to Alison, in time. She couldn't bear that. When she and Howell began to keep tryst, they would plot her escape, along with mine and Alison's.' She thought for a moment. 'If you wish, I will go back to last year, to the time when Eliza Dowling came to Ebbfield.'

At mention of that name I would have spoken, but quickly she stayed me. 'She did us no real harm. Yet she was our turnkey, brought in by my father to watch us. She knew what he did, but she would never go against him…' the hard look returned. 'In the end, she's a fool. He promised he would marry her, make her the new mistress of Ebbfield - but he had no such intent.'

'Will you speak of what came later?' I asked, reining in my anger. 'The time leading up to Susanna's death?'

At that, Jane became distressed; but again, she showed a strength that almost shamed me. 'I will, Master Justice,' she answered. 'For I come to the worst tragedy of all, that is still to be uncovered…' she drew a breath. 'And yet, it may be that you are the man who will see it through.'

I said nothing, only waited for her to continue. But when she did, it was all I could do not to exclaim aloud.

'I can tell you now why Susanna's body was not examined before the inquest,' Jane said, keeping her voice steady. 'For if it had been, it would be known that she was with child.'

I gave a start, my mind leaping ahead – but quickly she shook her head. 'It was not Howell's. How could it be, when they could only speak in haste, at a window? Now you begin to understand, I think.'

I was still, my eyes on her face; I had no words. That was how Childers and I heard the last part of her tale, sitting silently in my chamber, deaf to all else but her soft voice.

'It's what brought matters to the nub,' Jane said, her eyes downcast. 'And that's how, at last, Susanna found the courage to stand up to our father. That night is as fresh in my mind as if it were but an hour ago: how she fought him, screaming and crying, and how he shouted and railed at her in turn. Alison and I were locked in our chambers – by Dowling, of course – but we listened. We listened until we heard doors bang, then all was quiet.'

She looked up at me, her face pinched with emotion. 'I believed Susanna had fled from the house, how I do not know. All I know is that we never saw her again. And given where she was found, I fear they might even have taken her there.'

'*They* might have taken her?' I echoed.

'My father and Humphreys... did I not say that he too was there, that night?'

I stared at her, while several things fell into place: Dan Tait speaking of two men who used his boat... like a fool, I had not pressed him to tell who the other was, besides Cobbett. Ned Berritt's report of men by the Witching Pool, and the discovery of the girl's body next morning. Then I thought of Standish, and his apparent eagerness to bring about a suicide verdict – as he had done again in the matter of Howell Rhys. I recalled the father's face of anguish, and the promise I had made him.

I let out a sigh: at last, I believed I had my conspiracy. Had I been alone, I might have cried out in triumph.

'You poor girl... what wickedness you have suffered.'

It was Childers, regarding Jane in dismay. I could not recall seeing him shed a tear, but likely this was as close as he came. For her part, the girl merely returned his gaze.

'I believe I've told you all I can, Master Justice,' she said, turning to me.

'You have told enough,' I said, after a moment. 'Had I known…' I frowned as it struck me. 'Had I known such things were already occurring when I was a magistrate, I-'

'Nobody knew,' Jane said at once. 'Save those who shared my father's desires - or took payment for their silence.'

'Indeed… there seem to have been a number of those,' I said, feeling my anger rise anew. I thought back to what Boyd had told me of the first inquest, and what I had seen myself at the second – and on a sudden, I banged my hand on my chair.

'Like Justice Standish,' I muttered.

Childers gave a start. 'Sir, that's most-'

'I know what it is,' I snapped. 'But one way or another, I will lay the whole business bare, or…' I broke off; this was not something to air before Jane, who had told her story so bravely.

'You humble me with your courage,' I told her. 'You have done right – and again, I assure you that you are safe here. You and your sister may remain under my roof, for as long as you wish. Meanwhile…' I hesitated. 'Meanwhile, I need you to trust me to take what actions are needed.'

I paused, weighing my words, but the time was past for avoiding the facts. Meeting Jane's eye, I spelled it out.

'The matter is, we may be speaking of murder, mistress: the double murder of your sister and her unborn child. And there are the deaths of Howell Rhys and Ned Berritt, who were almost certainly murdered too - though as yet, I know not by whom. Hence, I must ask: are you willing to swear an oath as to what you have told me? And if you do, and the law takes its course, do you realise what the consequences might be?'

A moment passed, while Jane lowered her gaze. Childers and I exchanged looks, but it seemed there was no more to be said. Terrible crimes had been revealed, as wicked as any I had heard. For the present, I thought, there was only the word of this girl to set against that of her own father, one of the most powerful men in the shire… but perhaps that could change. For I knew who to confront next – and woe betide Abel Humphreys, if he should try using that fixed smile to disarm me again.

My train of thought was broken by Jane's quiet voice.

'I will do whatever is needed to bring justice, sir,' she said. 'For my sister, and for Howell... even the old woodman.' She sighed again. 'Indeed, I fear I will not sleep soundly until it is done, and we may lay the past to rest.'

At last, for the first time since her arrival, she managed a faint smile. It was brief, but it was enough.

EIGHTEEN

For the remainder of that day I remained alone in my private chamber, dwelling on Jane's testimony. Much was now clear, but it brought little comfort: the matter weighed upon me, and I could see no immediate source of aid. I dismissed Standish: he had questions to answer, but they would wait. I consoled myself somewhat in writing a letter to Boyd, giving him a full account of what had been revealed; Elkins would ride to Worcester and deliver it. Then came the difficult matter of informing Cobbett that his daughters were safe.

I confess I struggled over that, penning two versions of the letter before rejecting both. At last I decided to throw caution aside and tell him outright that the girls had sought my help, and were now lodged at Thirldon. I was uncertain what action he would take: given the kind of man he was, he might simply arrive in force and demand I hand them over. Or would he resort to the law, even accusing me of kidnapping? Hence, I took the decision to hold back the letter until the morrow. This day was the Sabbath, and I would wait before doing what I now burned to do: ride to Humphreys' farm and force a confession from him. The way my mind was working, I might have resorted to force, which is why I decided to take Childers with me.

'Once again,' I told him that evening, 'you will be my witness, as will Lockyer. We will be armed, but must draw no weapons. Leave the questioning to me. I mean to go early in the morning, and catch him unawares.'

He barely nodded; Jane's testimony that day had affected him deeply. 'And should you get some admission from Humphreys, what do you intend?' He asked. 'To take him by force?'

'I'm uncertain,' I admitted. 'In truth, my powers are no different from those of any gentleman. But I believe I have right on my side. Let's see what the day brings, shall we?'

Whereupon we parted, with my doing my best to appear calm and resolved. Yet I was in turmoil, and beset by doubt.

***

The day dawned fair, as the three of us got mounted and rode out of Thirldon. Hester was at the doors to see us leave; she was subdued, and had said little. Though she urged restraint on my part, she knew it was futile: she had always recognised my anger.

The way down to Powick was quiet, with few people about. I rode in front with Childers, the two of us wearing swords and poniards. Lockyer brought up the rear, armed with a dagger and an oak billet tied to his saddle. I had told him only as much as I needed to: that I intended to interrogate Humphreys for a suspected crime. He had taken in the news without expression, which caused me some disquiet: how much the Thirldon servants knew or speculated about our young guests, I did not know.

We clattered over the Teme bridge, and villagers stopped to observe us: an armed party, sober-faced and determined. In truth I felt like Justice Belstrang again, a magistrate with powers; whether Abel Humphreys would see it that way was a different matter. Yet matters would fall out, one way or another; and since the journey thereafter was quite short, it would be soon enough.

The farmyard was exactly as I had seen it last: untidy and deserted. Though the barn door was closed, and there was no-one watching. We rode up in a body, drew rein before the house and sat our horses in silence. But this time, nobody emerged.

A minute or more passed, and still all was quiet. Finally I dismounted, telling the others to do the same. Lockyer held the horses while Childers stood apart. Summoning my best authority, I strode to the house and knocked on the door.

At first there was no answer, though I fancied I heard sounds from within. Then came the scrape of a bolt being drawn, and at last the door opened - to reveal Mistress Humphreys in her black frock, gazing sightlessly past me.

'My husband's not here,' she snapped.

'It's Robert Belstrang, mistress,' I said, perhaps too loudly. 'Formerly Justice Belstrang. I was here ten days ago-'

'I remember,' came the terse reply. 'I may be blind, but I'm not a fool.'

'Then perhaps you'll tell me where he is.'

'I cannot.'

I paused, thinking on my next move, which irritated the woman. 'There's nothing for you here,' she said harshly – then she stiffened, as did I: there was a noise from within the house, as of a door closing. At once, I turned about.

'The rear!' I called to Childers. 'He's trying to flee.'

It was Lockyer who responded. Dropping the horses' reins, he moved quickly to the side of the house where there was a fence and, beyond that, an open paddock. Vaulting the bars with an alacrity that surprised me, he disappeared from sight. Meanwhile, Childers came forward to stand beside me.

'Will you accompany Mistress Humphreys inside?' I asked him. 'I fear she's not been entirely truthful with me.'

At that, the woman caught her breath and would have spoken – then she felt my hand on my arm, and went rigid.

'With your permission, madam,' I said, bending close. 'My servant is a gentleman... will you let him attend you?'

Leaving the two of them, I turned and made haste to follow Lockyer. I was unsure what to expect, but in the end the chase, if one could call it such, was short-lived. No sooner had I rounded the side of the farmhouse than the stout figure of Humphreys appeared, red-faced and out of breath, being marched forward by my servant.

'It's a while since I ran anywhere, Master Justice,' Lockyer said, breathing hard. 'But there was small need.' With a jerk of his head, he indicated his captive. 'The poor man is spent already.'

I waited until they were at the fence, noting with satisfaction that, this time, Humphreys' grin was noticeable by its absence. Panting, his thick tongue hanging loose, he regarded me with a mixture of fear and anger.

'Will you climb over?' I invited, placing a hand on my sword-hilt. 'Then we can enter your house by the main door. I'm eager to avail myself of your hospitality again.'

For a moment, it looked as if he would try to break free, but Lockyer was ready. Tightening his grip so that the man flinched, he spoke in his ear. 'You heard my master. Can you do it alone, or do you need my help?'

With a savage look, Humphreys put a hand on the top rail and prepared to get his portly frame over it.

***

The interrogation began badly.

'You have no right,' Humphreys protested, more than once. 'You're not a Justice, nor any officer of the law. I could charge you with trespass and affray, and more besides. I want you out of my house!'

'Believe me, nothing would give me more pleasure,' I told him, in my best magisterial tone. 'But let's have a talk first, shall we?'

He was about to reply, but instead threw a baleful look at Childers and I, facing him across his table. Lockyer had remained outside with the horses, but Mistress Humphreys was seated across the room. She had insisted on being present: an angry, silent figure, fists clenched in her lap.

'The young shepherd, Rhys,' I said, leaning forward abruptly. 'Did you kill him, or have someone else do it?'

Humphreys blinked in that owlish way of his, but gave no answer.

'Or what about Ned Berritt?' I continued. 'You once beat him severely, so I heard. Did you kill him too?'

There was a stir from across the room, as Sarah Humphreys shifted on her stool. Her husband had gone pale, but still said nothing.

'See now, I can take all day if need be,' I lied, fixing him with my blandest look. 'But I mean to have answers, which I can take to my friend Justice Standish in Worcester. Did I mention that he's most interested in the case, as are others?'

'What case?' Humphreys demanded then. 'I don't understand why you're here, charging me with these crimes-'

'I've laid no charges,' I broke in. 'I merely want to hear what you know of those deaths.' I paused, allowing a trace of anger to show. 'You see, I made a promise to the father of Howell Rhys, that I would try to find his son's killer. He doesn't believe Howell took his own life – and nor do I.'

'By God…' Humphreys swallowed, looking round for

something to drink, but the table was unladen. Meeting my eye briefly, he drew a breath, then: 'I swear on my father's grave, I did not kill him.'

'But you know who did,' I said, taking a gamble.

He said nothing; across the room, his wife sat motionless.

'Let's say it was Giles Cobbett who had him slain,' I suggested. 'After all, he'd threatened to do it. Though after his daughter's death, one might wonder at his motives - unless, that is, the youth knew things Cobbett didn't want spread abroad. I think you know what I speak of.'

Having said that, I sat back. I had touched on the topic of Cobbett's and Humphreys' treatment of Susanna sooner than intended, and was in danger of allowing my anger to burst forth. Catching Childers' eye, I saw that he thought the same.

'But I don't,' Humphreys said, shaking his head. 'Know what you speak of, I mean...'

'Please don't take me for a fool,' I retorted. 'Matters have come to light, concerning your frequent forays across the river to Ebbfield. Did you not know that the missing Cobbett girls have been found, and are being most helpful?'

The silence that fell then was deadly. I glanced briefly at the man's wife, who was still as a statue. Facing Humphreys again, I raised my eyebrows and waited.

'What is it you mean to do?' He asked, somewhat hoarsely. 'Were I to speak, I...' he gulped, and swallowed noisily. He was afraid now, as well he might be. 'I might have done things I regret,' he added, avoiding my eye. 'But murder is not one of them. I knew nothing of Rhys's death until he was found-'

'Tell him about Berritt!'

Sarah Humphreys' voice cut him short like a whipcrack. Startled, the three of us turned to see her on her feet, pointing a shaky finger at her husband. For his part Humphreys let out a moan, then slumped, his head in his hands.

'Damn you to hell,' he muttered. I looked from him to his wife, who at last gave vent to her feelings.

'You vile wretch - you worm!' She cried, taking a step forward. 'Do you think you can lie your way out of this, as you've lied all your miserable life? Make confession like a man, if you can remember how to behave as one!'

Trembling with rage, she jabbed her finger at him. Years of hatred and resentment, I realised, were spilling out – and all the while Humphreys remained still, his face hidden.

'Well now…' Taking a breath, I bent forward and seized the man's wrist, causing him to start. 'Will you not do as your wife bids, and tell me about Ned Berritt? I would prefer to see your lips move when you do.'

He lowered his hands, revealing a face haggard with fear.

'Or should I let her speak for you?' I enquired.

'No – let him condemn himself!'

Once again, Mistress Humphreys cried out. She took another step, until she was close to the table – and I swear her husband flinched, as if he believed she would strike him. It occurred to me that it might not be the first time that had happened… but she lowered her arm, and turned to me.

'He'll tell you what he did,' she said, breathing fast. 'For if he does not, he knows that I will.' Whereupon she waited as did we all, Childers and I looking hard at Humphreys… until at last, he made confession.

'I killed Berritt,' he admitted, in a voice so low he could barely be heard. 'I had to, or…'

'Or what?' I demanded.

He shook his head. 'I hired him to rid the farm of rats. He would never turn down the chance of a few pennies. He came in the afternoon… we cornered him in the barn, once he'd laid down that whoreson bow of his. It was easy enough.'

'Who's *we*?'

'My labourer and me. He knocked Berritt senseless, then we trussed him and took him upriver, after dark…'

'And threw him in, to drown,' I finished.

I met his eye, forcing him to look away. But I had my confession now, and I meaned to draw every last scrap of intelligence from him.

'His body was supposed to wash downstream, was it not?' I persisted. 'Save that the water's somewhat low, so it got caught in an eddy and fetched up in the reeds. Which is where Dan Tait came in, was it not?'

He continued to avoid my gaze – but at the mention of Tait, a sickly look appeared.

'So, at last we have it,' I sighed, with no small relief. 'Berritt was an unwanted witness at the inquest: the finder of the body, who could make difficulties for your landlord. Which is why I assume it was on Cobbett's orders that you despatched the fellow.' I paused, then: 'Not that it matters, for you'll stand trial for his murder. I promise you that.'

There was a movement then - but not from Humphreys, who slumped like the beaten man he was. I looked round to see his wife step back to her stool, and sit down heavily.

'May God forgive him,' she murmured. 'For I cannot.'

'No… you could never forgive, could you?'

Like an animal her husband turned upon her, his voice a savage snarl.

'Not me,' he cried, 'nor the miscarried children, nor our grasping landlord – not a soul, could you ever forgive! The whole world must pay for your misery, and not be allowed to forget! And whatever I did, it was never enough! Would that the God you claim to worship could pay you out for what I've endured – to the devil with your whoreson piety! Now I'll be gone from here, and you can stew in your own hatred until you die! At least I'll never have to listen to your whining voice again!'

Whereupon he fell back, and said not another word.

Nor would he, until he was taken away tied to his horse, destined for the prison in Worcester. His rogue of a labourer, I would learn, had already fled, paid off for his silence.

As for Humphreys' other crimes, the wicked abuse of Susanna Cobbett in collusion with her father: I decided to spare his wife that part of my interrogation. She too was broken, I knew, though she refused to show her feelings. She would say nothing further to me or my servants. In silence she let us leave while remaining seated, in a corner of the room where the sunlight did not reach.

The last part of Humphreys' confession took place on our return journey, away from prying eyes at the quietest spot I knew: the Witching Pool.

NINETEEN

It was mid-morning by the time we arrived at the edge of Newland Wood, where I drew rein and bade Childers and Lockyer dismount. Humphreys was left on his horse with hands bound before him, while the three of us gathered in a close group. On the journey I had told Lockyer what I intended, which meant letting him know something of Humphreys' crimes. He listened closely, then frowned.

'In truth, sir, I've heard rumours about him,' he said. 'Never paid much mind to them, but...' he tensed. 'That's why the Cobbett maids sought safety with you, is it?'

I met his gaze, but said nothing. Whereupon, with a shake of his head, he stepped away and returned to the horses. When he looked up at Humphreys, the man quickly turned from him.

'What do you mean to do here?' Childers asked me, with a glance at our captive. 'Threaten to drown him?'

'I hadn't thought of that,' I said. 'But I need to sweat him enough to incriminate Cobbett. Hence, I will allow my anger to boil over. Your task will be to restrain me, until we've put the fear of God into the man. Can you do that?'

His reply was a curt nod. Whereupon we gathered about Humphreys and helped him down from the saddle – somewhat roughly, I confess. Once on the ground, he began to shake.

'What does this mean?' He demanded. 'You said we were going to Worcester...'

'Did I?' I replied. 'Well, just now I want you to take a walk with me and my steward. If your legs hold up, that is.'

He would have protested, but saw it would avail him nothing. Leaving Lockyer with the horses, Childers and I frog-marched the man through the trees until we reached the Witching Pool. As I expected, there was no-one about. Cobbett's man Mount, who had turned me away the last time I was here, had left his service, according to Tait: just another minion, it seemed, paid for his silence and sent packing.

'Here we are,' I said, as cheerfully as I could. We stopped near the edge of the pool, its surface dark and still but for an occasional ripple from the breeze. 'How long is it since you were here, I wonder?'

The question was for Humphreys, who wet his fleshy lips, eyes darting about as if seeking a means of escape.

'I pray you, be at ease,' I told him, letting go of his arm. At my signal Childers did the same, the two of us standing together to face him.

'We're all men here, are we not?' I went on. 'So why don't you tell us about the Cobbett girls, and what you liked to do with them? I speak particularly of Susanna, who met her tragic end at this very place, as you'll recall.'

The man threw me a fearful look, then lowered his gaze.

'And her young swain, too,' I continued. 'The shepherd, beaten and dragged away from his flock - poison forced down his throat, I heard. Then dumped in the water, so it would look as if he'd tried to join his lost love in spirit.'

'In God's name, what do you want of me?' Humphreys blurted. Sweat showed on his brow, as he tugged uselessly at his bonds. 'I swore to you, I know nothing of that.'

'You did,' I agreed. 'As you've kindly admitted to the murder of the woodman who roamed hereabouts. So, we'll go back to Susanna Cobbett, shall we?'

The man swallowed, his gaze flitting from me to Childers, who regarded him stonily. 'See now,' he began, somewhat breathlessly, 'if you mean to implicate me in her death somehow, you are utterly mistaken. I was a friend to those girls – almost an uncle! I would never harm any of them...'

'You're lying, you vermin,' I broke in, with a swift glance at Childers: it was time for a performance. 'You used her like a whore, as you would have done her sisters. Chattels, to serve your twisted desires...' Raising my voice, I took a step towards him and put a hand to my sword.

'In truth,' I snapped, 'I've a mind to end your miserable life here and now. Tell Standish you tried to escape, and attacked me - what could I do but defend myself? I have a witness to speak for me... have I not?' I turned to Childers, who nodded at once.

'You have, sir,' he said. 'But I urge you to master your feelings and let the law take its course. This man faces the gallows already, so-'

'Yes, yes,' I answered testily, making a show of reining in my anger. 'But then again...' I fixed Humphreys with my hardest expression. 'I'd sorely like to deal him a few cuts for good measure. We can say he put up a struggle.'

'God in heaven...' Eying each of us in turn, Humphreys almost swayed on his feet. 'Have mercy, I beg you!'

'You do what?' With a quick movement, I put hand to belt and drew my poniard. It had barely left the scabbard in years, and would likely cut naught but cheese, though Humphreys could not know that. When I held it up, his mouth fell open in terror.

'Have mercy, did you say?' I lunged forward, put the poniard to the man's neck and held it there until he quaked. Childers, meanwhile, appeared to forget that I was acting and hurried to seize my arm.

'Master Justice, stay yourself!' He shouted.

I ignored him. 'You dare to ask for mercy?' I snapped at Humphreys. 'How often did Susanna do so? How many times did she beg to be spared your depravity, yours and her father's? And that night, when she dared to stand up to him in her anguish - when she knew she was carrying his child - you were there, weren't you? Did you silence her, or did Cobbett? Answer me, or I'll-'

'He strangled her!'

Humphreys' cracked voice, filled with fear, rang out in the wood, startling both my steward and I. It startled a few birds too, sending them scattering from the treetops. Lowering the poniard, I drew back, even as Childers let go of me. The pair of us gazed at the man, who had just given me the confession I needed, though I was stunned by its substance. We could only watch as, all resistance spent, he suddenly fell to his knees and began to weep.

'She fought him,' he sobbed. 'Until he lost all restraint... it was done in a rage. I could never have committed such an act... whatever else I did...'

He broke off and gave way to tears, while all I could do was turn away, drawing long breaths. I too was sweating, I realised, droplets running from my brow. Absently, I sheathed the poniard and looked at Childers, who was aghast.

'His daughter?' He murmured, meeting my gaze. 'Cobbett slew his own child?'

I made no answer. After a while I turned to regard Humphreys: as abject a figure as I ever saw, crouching like one facing execution - which in time, he would.

'So,' I managed at last, 'the girl was already dead when she left Ebbfield - but you helped take her body away.'

He barely nodded, his face to the ground.

'You took her to Tait's Crossing, where the ferryman waited,' I continued, looking down at him.

'No - Cobbett roused Tait, and told him we needed his boat.' Humphreys turned his head towards me, speaking hoarsely. 'She was wrapped in a bundle, tied across a horse... I stayed back while Cobbett struck his bargain. The ferryman left us to make the crossing... he didn't see her body.'

That, at least, came to me as a relief. Tait was a villainous old goat, I thought, but he was not an accomplice to Susanna's murder – unlike the man kneeling before me. In no uncertain terms, I spelled it out for him: just another crime to add to the charges. His response was only silence.

'Well now...' drawing a long breath, I took a step towards him. 'I do believe you've told me all you need, for now. You and Cobbett took his daughter's body across the river, brought her here and did your best to make it look as if she'd drowned herself. And since no-one examined the body, nothing could be said about strangulation. Your landlord has been most thorough in covering his tracks, has he not?'

'Meanwhile,' I continued, 'a culprit had to be found - a scapegoat, whom Cobbett wished to be rid of. Save that it's more difficult to blame Agnes Mason for the death of Rhys, since she was already imprisoned. Yet the youth had to be removed – and you still swear you were not involved in that?'

'By the Christ, I do!'

His face red and puffy, Humphreys looked round suddenly. 'I

never went near him! Damn you, I've confessed to taking Berritt's life - what would it avail me to deny another killing? The result will be the same, will it not?'

Once again, he slumped and turned away; but he was right, and I had no cause to disbelieve him. Pondering the matter, I knew that Cobbett still had the most compelling motive to do away with Howell Rhys – but that would have to wait.

'I think we're done here, sir, are we not?'

Childers was eying me, his distaste for the whole business evident. Seeing his eagerness to be gone, I could only agree. I was on the point of asking him to help me drag our prisoner to his feet, when:

'Parson Woollard,' I said, as the notion occurred. 'I had almost forgotten… what's the nature of your relations with him?'

Humphreys stirred. 'What do you mean, relations?' he muttered. 'I had none, save slight acquaintance.'

'The funeral,' I said. 'By Susanna Cobbett's grave… I watched you when no-one else did. I saw how you smiled, as I know something of Woollard's practices. Tell me - was he another of Cobbett's wicked circle?'

There was a moment, then the man let out a bitter laugh, more like a bark.

'He would sorely have liked to be,' he spat. 'That fool… he was naught but Cobbett's instrument, kept to do his bidding with promises that would never be honoured. You speak of a circle? There was none, but the landlord and I…'

On a sudden he reared himself, tugging at his bonds as if he could tear them asunder.

'Enough!' He shouted. 'I've told all, and put my head in the noose – and I swear to God, death will be a release! Now take me away from here, or throw me in the whoreson pool to drown – for I no longer care a fig!'

And those were the last words I would hear him speak.

**

To return to Thirldon after such a day, with its air of tranquillity, was a blessed relief.

It was evening, and I had done all that I could do: delivered

Humphreys to the prison in Worcester, and sworn out a warrant against him for the murder of Ned Berritt. I would write a report, I told the sergeant-at-arms, and send copies to all those I could think of including Standish. Having rid ourselves of our burden, my servants and I rode out of the city, crossed the bridge and took the homeward road with lighter hearts. Within the hour I was at supper, tired and saddened, but ready to tell Hester what had occurred. Childers, for once, was not present. Pleading an aching head, he had excused himself and gone to bed. Hester offered to send a supper to his chamber, but he had refused.

'The girls are abed too,' she said, as we sat with cups of sack. 'They have been together all day.'

'Did you speak with them?'

'A little. On one thing, they are both adamant: they will never return to Ebbfield. Jane swore to me that if we tried to send her home, she would run away. While Alison assured me that she would rather die.'

I heaved a sigh: somehow, I had to tell the sisters what had befallen Susanna, since they appeared to be uncertain. It would be one of the hardest things I had to do.

'They'll stay here for the present, of course,' I said. 'But in time, other arrangements must follow. Perhaps they can be made Wards of Court.'

'They spoke of relatives in Gloucester,' Hester said. 'On their mother's side, I should say.'

'Yet in the meantime, I must inform Cobbett of their whereabouts,' I told her. 'I can't delay it any longer - indeed, he may know already.'

She nodded, and reached out to place her hand on mine. 'This has been an ordeal for you. I fear I was not always approving of your actions, but you have brought justice for Susanna.'

'Not yet,' I answered, with a shake of my head. 'Bringing a charge of murder against a man like Giles Cobbett will not be easy. The only witness is Humphreys, and I cannot count on him when the matter comes to trial – assuming it does. The wretch has nothing left to lose.'

'Can you be certain that Humphreys was the only witness?' Hester queried. 'Surely there were servants who saw him depart, with the body shrouded as it was?'

I gave a snort. 'They wouldn't dare go against him - not even the nurse. She worships the man, from what I can see.'

We were silent then, each of us pondering the matter, whereupon on a sudden, I thought of Boyd. It was four days since I had last seen him, though it seemed longer.

'See now, why should I not press for a new inquest, on Susanna?' I said. 'New evidence has emerged which Childers and I can swear to. Boyd and I could go to Standish and demand it – if he refused, I could threaten to go over his head.'

Despite my weariness, I had brightened somewhat. Should Standish be unwilling to entertain the notion, it would look suspicious. I knew he favoured Cobbett, hence he might appear to be trying to cover up his daughter's death. But given what we now knew…

'I suppose you are right,' Hester said then. 'And, if you would hear my counsel, it would be to cease going off on any further missions of dubious legality - questioning people and so forth - and let the law prevail. In short, put aside your feelings concerning Standish, and take the whole matter to him.'

I met her gaze, but on a sudden I was filled with doubt. Given my relations with the Justice, matters could easily turn unpleasant, even ending in disarray. Though I knew I could count on Boyd as a voice of reason, if he would be my witness.

'Well, you too are right,' I said at last. 'I'll send messages first thing tomorrow, and be in Worcester by mid-day…' I sighed. 'After I have told Jane and Alison what I've uncovered.'

'We will tell them together,' Hester said.

TWENTY

The next day, I had barely left Thirldon on my way to Worcester when a new resolve formed: I would go once again to the Guildhall to visit Agnes Mason.

Despite all that had happened – or indeed, because of all that had happened – I had a strong desire to see her. *In primis*, I would inform her that matters were moving at last in her favour, even if I could not assure her of imminent release; and *secundus*, I might satisfy myself that she was not being maltreated. I was unaware how matters stood just now in the city. And as I rode, suspicions arose again about who might have arranged for that paper to be nailed to the doors of the minster. All trails now seemed to lead back to the one who had begun this whole affair: Giles Cobbett, a man I now burned to see arrested.

It was approaching mid-day when I entered the city, walking Leucippus slowly through the bustling throng. By now, I had striven to put behind me the distressing hour Hester and I had spent with Jane and Alison, in which I told them the circumstances of their sister's death. We had expected them to be distraught, and so they were, but in the last moments I spent with them, some degree of calm seemed to have settled. I left them in tears, hugging one another, while Hester remained to offer what comfort she could.

Hence, it would be untruthful of me to say that I approached the task ahead with dispassion. I feared my anger would triumph once I faced Standish again. But I hoped to have Boyd as my hand of restraint: I had sent Elkins early with a letter, giving the good doctor a fuller account of events. In this frame of mind, having found a horse-holder, I walked to his house and made my presence known. Boyd's servant admitted me, then coughed to gain my attention.

'If I might make bold, Master Justice,' he said quietly, 'I should tell you that the doctor is out of sorts. There has been an incident.'

I paused. 'What manner of incident?'

'I think it best he tells you himself.'

I entered Boyd's parlour, hat in hand, and he rose to greet me... whereupon I stopped in mid-stride. There was a large purple bruise on his temple.

'What in God's name has happened to you?' I asked.

'Well might you wonder,' he replied, in dour tones. 'You could say that the wound is a result of your request, to visit your incarcerated friend at the Guildhall.'

In consternation, I returned his gaze. 'What, was there an affray?'

'After a fashion. I told you that feelings are running high. People gather outside, and anyone who visits the witch – or Mother Blackcat, as they've dubbed her – is suspect. In short, a handful of ruffians jostled and insulted me, to the point where I was obliged to draw sword. Several missiles were thrown – the evidence of which you see.'

He sat down, gesturing me to do the same.

'You poor fellow,' I murmured. 'I can but ask your pardon-'

'You need not trouble yourself,' Boyd broke in. 'For what I have to tell you is somewhat unpleasant.' He waited until I was seated, then: 'It seems Mason has not refused food – not entirely. She takes a little.' He paused, then added with a frown: 'Though there's a jailer who appears to enjoy watching her suffer. I do not know his name-'

'Burton,' I snapped. 'By heaven, I'll make him pay.'

The doctor sighed, then fumbled on his side-table and held up what I saw was my recent letter.

'What a wicked and tawdry business you have uncovered,' he said. And when I barely nodded: 'I have given it some thought, yet I'm uncertain what is the best course of action. Do you still mean to go to Standish?'

'Of course,' I replied. 'He's both Magistrate and acting Coroner. And he knows I will not let the matter rest, but call on other authorities if I must. Whatever his relations with Cobbett, he will be damaged by association. He has to act, or appear to be at fault himself.'

'And you believe you have enough evidence to accuse Cobbett of murder?'

'I do.'

He was silent for a while, whereupon I asked him if he had seen Agnes in person. He shook his head.

'I was not permitted. However, I spoke with one or two people I know, and the sergeant-at-arms. When I told him that I came at your behest, he was willing to talk.' A frown forming, he added: 'The man seemed ill-at-ease. I believe he might even suspect that Mason is innocent of the charges.'

I thought on that, before broaching the matter that now troubled me. 'In view of what's happened, I cannot ask you to come with me to Standish,' I said. 'I've involved you more than I had right to.'

'Well now, as I recall,' my friend said, 'I asked you to keep me informed of the case, as I was more than willing to accompany you to Ebbfield that day. And now...' a wry look appeared. 'I heartily dislike being told to keep my nose out. This is a matter of principle and of justice - moreover, I too have a reputation in this city.' He paused for a moment, then: 'Hence, I will be your witness when you confront Standish. And I will request that a new inquest be held into Susanna Cobbett's death. But I pray you, don't ask me to visit Mistress Mason again.'

I gave a sigh; I was both relieved and resolved. 'No... that's something I must do myself. And if I return here in an hour, would you be ready to accompany me to the Justice's house?'

He indicated assent, then lowered his gaze. 'That Woolland – what a vile excuse for a parson,' he muttered. 'I should have been less courteous with him, that day in Kempsey.'

He looked up, and fixed me with a gaze which was enough to spur me on: onwards to what I hoped was the last phase of this whole, tragic affair. Determined, but with some trepidation, I left his house and made my way directly to the Guildhall.

But once inside, I was forbidden to descend to the cellars.

'I have my orders, Master Justice,' Sergeant Lisle told me, the two of us standing by the stairhead. 'And this time, I fear I cannot make exception. The woman is to be left alone until she comes to trial.' He paused, then added in a low voice: 'It's feared she will bewitch anyone who goes near. There's even been a rumour that she might call on demons, to whisk her away.'

'God in heaven...' I raised my eyes. 'Cannot I even speak to her through the door?'

In his customary stolid fashion, Lisle shook his head.

I considered, wondering if I might take this man whom I trusted into my confidence, in part at least. Instead, I asked him how Agnes appeared.

'In truth, sir, she is restless,' he answered. 'I fear that, by the time she comes to trial, she will be in a sorry state.'

I faced him squarely. 'It may be that matters will turn out otherwise,' I said. 'I have evidence that I intend to put before Justice Standish.'

But when the man raised his brows, I reined in my impulse to say more. With a heavy heart, I left him and got myself out into the street. Only then did I observe a small knot of people gathered near the doors, eying me suspiciously. Doubtless they had been there when I arrived... was I so intent on seeing Agnes again that I had failed to notice them? One or two eyed me in belligerent fashion – and on a sudden I halted.

'I know you, do I not?' I said.

The man I was looking at returned my gaze – whereupon recognition dawned on him, too. Before me stood one of the two who had stopped me at the Witching Pool that day. One, I now knew, was William Mount, who had disappeared after testifying at the inquest into Howell Rhys... and here was the other.

'I think not, sir,' he said, rather quickly.

'Indeed?' I moved closer, which caused the others – idlers, for the most part – to step back. 'Let me refresh your memory. It was at the Witching Pool, where you kept guard. You serve Giles Cobbett, do you not?'

At that there was a stir from the other men, several of them wearing puzzled looks. But the one I addressed shook his head.

'Nay sir, I do not.' And he would have walked off, had I not placed hand on sword and summoned my best authority.

'Wait,' I ordered.

He stopped, glanced at his companions who were beginning to move away, then eyed me warily.

'See now, I've a mind to have you arrested,' I told him,

finding myself exhilarated at having someone to punish. 'I'm a private citizen, of course, and I'm unsure of the charge as yet, but I'll think of something.'

He stiffened, then by instinct his hand went to the poniard at his belt.

'That will serve,' I said at once. 'Threatening a gentleman and former Justice.' For good measure I drew my sword part-way, leaving a few inches in the scabbard.

'Nay, I…' the man swallowed. 'I do not threaten, sir…'

He stopped, finding himself suddenly alone. A few bystanders had gathered out of curiosity, but kept their distance. Seizing the moment, I drew close enough to make him start.

'Give me some answers – truthful ones - and I'll forget I saw you,' I said, speaking low. 'First, do you serve Cobbett or do you not?'

He hesitated, then managed a slight nod.

'In that case, what do you do in Worcester?' I demanded. 'Let me guess: your master told you stir up trouble. To gather a few loafers, buy them a drink, then lead them to the Guildhall to cry out against Agnes Mason. Am I near the mark?'

He gulped, but it was answer enough – whereupon another thought struck me. 'By the Christ – was it you who tacked that paper to the minster doors, calling for her death?'

The man caught his breath and made no answer, but it made little difference. Matters were clear in my mind now - as they had been, I realised, for a good while. I even broke into a smile of triumph, which seemed to alarm my victim even more.

'I'm but a servant, sir,' he blurted, 'and can do no other than what I'm ordered.' He was beginning to blabber, which for me had always been a token of guilt. 'Everyone fears the witch - do not you? And if my master's eager to bring about her end, what man wouldn't be, when she caused the death of his daughter? I swear, I'd hang her myself if I could-'

That was as far as he got before I lost all restraint. Thrusting my sword back into the scabbard, I seized the varlet by the throat. 'Shut your foul mouth,' I breathed. 'Were you not such a dolt, I'd wring your neck where you stand. As for your master…' I caught my breath. 'Your master's a murderous

140

tyrant, who will end his days on a scaffold. Now get out of my sight – leave Worcester, and take yourself back to Ebbfield. More, take my advice and leave there before the manor falls into other hands – for you may find you've no place left.'

With a shove I sent him reeling backwards, causing a muttering from the watchers. I had caused a stir, which was the last thing I needed just then. And yet, I took some satisfaction in seeing Cobbett's man turn and make haste to lose himself, head lowered. I watched him disappear around the nearest corner, then let out a breath.

There was some time yet before I was due to return to Boyd's house, which suited me well enough. I needed a drink; or perhaps, with the prospect of confronting Standish ahead of me, more than one might be better.

***

An hour later the two of us stood in the doorway of the Justice's house, hearing his servant protest that his master was too busy to see anyone.

'He will see me,' I said firmly. 'I have vital evidence to put before him, of a capital crime.'

'Master Belstrang, I pray you…' the man wore a pained look. 'In truth, since your last visit the Justice has given me instructions not to admit you. He is weighed down with business-'

'As am I,' I broke in. 'But this will not wait. Now stand aside, or I'll-'

'You will what?' Came a voice from the rear, causing the servant to turn about. Standish himself was shuffling along the hallway towards us, wearing his familiar scowl.

'Am I ever to be free of you, Belstrang?' He sighed. 'Pray state the purpose of your visit, and let me-'

'It's murder,' I said at once, causing him to stop in his tracks. Holding up the report I had prepared, I made bold to step forward. 'Do you wish me to read it aloud, here and now?'

A moment passed, in which the Justice appeared to notice Boyd for the first time. A wary look appeared, but it was clear that he had little choice but to hear us. With another sigh, he dismissed his servant and bade us follow him indoors.

No sooner were we in his closet, however, and he had retreated behind his cluttered table, than he became brusque. 'What do you mean by presenting yourself in this precipitate manner, sir?' He snorted. 'If you have evidence of such a serious nature, why have you not sent…'

He stopped, a look of doubt on his features. Following his gaze, I experienced some relief at sight of my last letter to him, lying atop a pile of papers. With a flourish, I threw my new report down in front of him.

'It's all here,' I told him. 'I suggest you read it most carefully, along with the missive I sent. Have you troubled yourself to read that yet?' Whereupon, taking his silence for a negative, I managed a thin smile. 'Please do so,' I added. 'Meanwhile, the doctor and I will wait outside.'

It took him more than a quarter of an hour, during which time Boyd and I made ourselves comfortable in the main room of the house. During this time the Justice's wife appeared, she who had accosted Hester in the street more than a week ago, I recalled. But when Boyd and I stood up to greet her, she disappeared with barely a nod.

'It seems courtesy isn't a priority in this house,' my friend observed drily. 'Or perhaps it's merely because you are *persona non grata* here.'

I was about to make reply, but the sound of a door opening stayed me. Justice Standish stood at the entrance to his chamber, wearing a look which I might describe as one of angry dismay. At once, we rose to face him.

'You had better come in here,' he said.

TWENTY-ONE

Standish was shaken, yet he was still defiant. He now knew all that I had uncovered, though it seemed he had not yet been told of Humphreys being taken to the prison.

'I had no knowledge of that man's activities,' he said, shaking his head.

'Nor of Cobbett's?' I asked, somewhat sharply.

'I would swear to it.' He glanced at Boyd, who was eying him without expression. 'I suppose your concern, doctor, is that of the inquest once more?' He enquired. 'I fear you're somewhat late in that regard…'

'If you mean an inquest into the death of the man Berritt, sir, you're mistaken,' Boyd said at once. 'I'm here to press for a new inquest into the death of Susanna Cobbett.'

Standish frowned, opened his mouth, then closed it again, whereupon I added my opinion that a new inquest into the death of Howell Rhys should also be held. But to that he shook his head again, more firmly.

'It isn't possible. You were there when the verdict was given – it cannot be changed.'

'Not even in the light of new evidence? I enquired.

'What new evidence?' On a sudden, the man went on the attack. 'I'll allow you have brought grave charges against Giles Cobbett, though nothing substantial in regard to Rhys's death. And in my opinion, you have acted beyond the law in conducting these enquiries. Once again, I must remind you that you're no longer Justice Belstrang. Moreover, in taking Cobbett's daughters under your roof as you have, you might incur a charge of abduction – had you not considered that?'

'You've read my account of what the man did,' I retorted. 'Would you truly wish to return those maids to his house?'

'I…' to my surprise, Standish faltered. 'What powers do I have to tell him how to treat his daughters?' he muttered. 'Moreover, they cannot testify against him – nor are they witnesses to the death of their sister. Your only witness, in fact, appears to be Humphreys. Hardly the most reliable sort, would you not agree?'

I caught Boyd's eye, struggling to contain myself. Was the man about to refuse to act? It was intolerable.

'Perhaps - but then, all other potential witnesses are either dead or have flown the coop,' I replied. 'Ned Berritt, Cobbett's man Mount, who lied at the inquest-'

'That's enough, Belstrang,' the Justice snapped. 'You go too far, as always.'

'By heaven, you're taking Cobbett's side,' I exclaimed, my restraint crumbling. 'Indeed, you've aided him all along, have you not? Shaped both inquests to produce verdicts of suicide, done nothing to allay rumours of witchcraft... you're determined to see Agnes Mason convicted, and have been from the start! Now I wish I'd-'

'Robert.' In agitation, Boyd turned on me. 'I urge you...'

'No, save your breath!'

Standish was on his feet, eyes blazing, as we had faced each other in this room before. Raising a hand, he pointed it at me – and to my surprise, it shook a little.

'Let him spew his vile accusations!' he cried. 'He's eager to damage me, and has been ever since I took his place as magistrate. Is it not so, Belstrang? I dare you to deny it!'

For a moment I made no reply; the meeting had turned out as I feared, and I was at least partly to blame. Drawing a breath, I looked down at my own report, still spread out on Standish's table... whereupon a notion flew up from somewhere, and found its way into words.

'Perhaps I should have mentioned that there is further evidence, which I've chosen to withhold until now,' I said, summoning my bland look. 'I was hoping you might act rightly and move to arrest Cobbett, this very day. But since you appear unwilling, I'm forced to keep it to myself.'

Silence fell. Boyd's eyes flitted from me to Standish and back while the Justice, still on his feet, was breathing hard. I could read his thoughts: was Belstrang bluffing, or...

'You lie,' he said at last. But he sat down, somewhat heavily.

'I beg your pardon?' I threw back, my heart thudding. 'Do

you truly wish to accuse me of lying? If so, I'll have no choice but to demand satisfaction…'

'In God's name!' Boyd spoke up in exasperation. 'This has become a comedy. Duelling's unlawful, and-'

'So it is, in theory,' Standish broke in, his eyes fixed on mine. 'The King disapproves strongly, and has legislated against it. But men with a grievance can always resort to a quiet place, and settle matters between themselves.' He turned his gaze on Boyd. 'Perhaps you will be called upon to be this man's witness in somewhat different circumstances?'

'I'll be a party to no such thing, sir,' Boyd retorted. 'And I confess to a deep disappointment to see two magistrates – or one magistrate and one former – demeaning themselves in this manner. We are in knowledge of terrible crimes. Can you not put rivalries aside, and look to the matter in hand?'

He paused and looked at each of us in turn. 'I speak of justice, sirs - or had you forgotten?'

My friend fell silent, but it was enough to shame me. Then, he had oft acted as my conscience. I threw him a look of approval, and waited. The silence dragged on, but Boyd's words had proved effectual. Somewhat chastened, Standish gazed down at my report without seeing it, then finally looked up.

'I will set things in motion, to bring Giles Cobbett in for questioning,' he said quietly.

'And what of Humphreys?' I asked.

'He will be questioned too, of course.'

I tried not to show my relief. For there were matters yet untangled, that weighed on me still.

'The parson, Woolland,' I said.

'What of him?' Standish demanded, with a look of suspicion. 'Do you claim you knew nothing of his activities too?'

'Most assuredly I do.' The man was growing angry again. 'And are you presuming to interrogate me now? You stretch license to its limits, Belstrang…'

'Your pardon,' I broke in, managing to contain myself. 'But I was somewhat surprised to see you in private conversation with the man that morning in Powick, after the inquest. Mistress Dowling was there too, as I recall.'

Another of those moments passed, in which Standish seemed to be torn between making some dry response or losing his temper. This time he chose the former.

'Mistress Dowling is an acquaintance, nothing more,' he said in a flat tone. 'As for Woolland...' he allowed a frown to appear. 'Since you are so concerned, I will tell you in confidence. I offered him some advice: to quit his living and depart for some other place, while he still had the chance.'

I met his gaze, but saw no guile... was there even a hint of disgust? But I believed the man, which brought some further relief. If I had harboured the least suspicion that Standish too shared Woollard's and Cobbett's tastes, I would have struggled in vain to contain my anger.

'Well, he has heeded your advice,' I said. 'He assured Mistress Cobbett that he would never be seen again.'

Standish said nothing, but sat back and lowered his gaze. On a sudden he looked tired, and in no mood for further debate. It was time to leave: I caught Boyd's eye, and signalled assent. But there was one thing more: a burning desire that I would not leave unaired.

'Who will you send to bring Cobbett in?' I asked. 'Sergeant Lisle, and others?'

'It's likely he will be given the order,' he replied... whereupon he sat up sharply. 'I hope you're not proposing to go along too? That would seem to be a matter of vengeance, given your sympathy for Cobbett's daughters. I cannot-'

'Allow it?' I broke in. 'Well, I fail to see on what grounds you can prevent me. I'm a private citizen with an interest-'

'Nay sir, you overstep yourself,' Standish broke in. 'You may in time be called as a witness, and-'

'I will relish that,' I said, becoming heated again. 'Yet I might remind you that I spoke of certain matters known to me alone, that touch on this whole affair. One of them...' I paused, aware of Boyd groaning under his breath, but blundered on; I was determined, and would not be gainsaid.

'One of them is an account of certain men who have enjoyed secret stipends from Giles Cobbett, to further his aims,' I finished. 'I name no names – as yet.'

It was a bluff, of course; but sometimes even a Justice may be susceptible to what I term the *Minatio Celata* - the Veiled Threat. Standish had stiffened, struggling to appear calm, but I saw it at last.

He was in Cobbett's pay – and he suspected that I knew it. Henceforth, I had a notion he would be more amenable to any request I might make of him; the notion gave me quiet satisfaction.

'I will make request of you,' I said. 'Might I be permitted to offer support in the arrest of Giles Cobbett, when the party sets out for Ebbfield? As a former Justice myself I deem it a public duty... can we agree on that, at least?'

I waited, allowing him to read my gaze in any way he liked, until at last came the answer I sought.

'Go, then - ride with Lisle,' Standish said, in a voice of weariness. 'It's clear you mean to do so anyway, as you have striven to wear me down from the moment you arrived here. Indeed...' he paused, nodding slowly. 'I think in your heart you intend to take revenge on me too, by any means you can. In which case, Belstrang, you will find me equal to the match – whether it be at sword-point, or in a court of law. For now, I have business to conduct – are you content?'

My answer was a polite nod, and soon afterwards Boyd and I left his house.

It would be some time before I was in Standish's company again. But the burr that chafed me remained, and doubtless it chafed him too. There would be a reckoning between us, some day; it was but a matter of where, and when.

TWENTY-TWO

The arrest of Giles Cobbett was set for the following day, on another breezy morning, about nine of the clock.

The party was led by Sergeant Lisle for the Crown, on a warrant from Justice Standish. He was accompanied by three constables armed with horse pistols. I had brought Elkins and Lockyer with me, for my own reassurance more than anything else. That made the party seven in number, well-mounted and determined. Having spent a restless night, I was taut with apprehension, not least because Cobbett's daughters were still under my roof, and were fearful of what the day might bring. I had been obliged to tell them their father was to be taken to Worcester prison, which brought little comfort.

We rode in silence along the south road, attracting stares from people travelling to the city. Lisle and I had exchanged a few words on setting out, but he was in no mood to talk. On a few occasions I caught him glancing my way, as if he was uneasy about my presence. Yet the journey was short, and without incident. We passed Tait's Crossing, where the boat had been pulled up on the riverbank. The ferryman, as so often, was not to be seen. And a short while later we were approaching Ebbfield, where the first surprise awaited us: the narrow bridge across the moat had been blocked with bundles of cordage, boards and logs.

The party reined in warily, but there was no-one in sight. Walking Leucippus forward, I halted beside Lisle.

'Well, Master Justice,' he said. 'You know Cobbett better than most here, I'd wager. What think you of this?'

'I'm unsure,' I answered. 'It almost looks as if he expects a siege. One might think we're back in the time of the Wars of the Roses, moat and all...' I indicated the water, which was foul and weed-choked. 'Though, since a man could wade across, it's not much of a defence.'

'Nor is that barricade,' Lisle said. 'Will your servants lend a hand to demolish it?'

The operation was soon in train. As the constables, along with Elkins and Lockyer, pulled apart the crude barrier and threw most of it into the water, it occurred to me that this was some delaying tactic on the part of Cobbett. It made me wary: the man had now been informed of the whereabouts of his daughters, yet had made no effort to bring them home. Was he planning something?

If he was, we would soon discover its nature. Within a short time the party was mounted again, clattering over the bridge and under the gatehouse arch into the cobbled courtyard which, as I had somehow expected, was deserted.

We halted and sat our mounts, but no-one appeared. After a moment Lisle got down, signalling to his men to do the same. My own servants eased their mounts close to mine.

'I don't like this, sir,' Lockyer said.

'Nor do I,' I told him. 'But we'd best wait and watch.'

Lisle was walking to the door of the manor, the constables behind him. There was no sign of life at the windows; nor, I realised, was there smoke from any chimneys. In fact, the manor appeared abandoned. I had a notion to check the stables, but turned as Lisle reached the door and proceeded to knock hard upon it.

'Giles Cobbett!' He called loudly. 'You are to accompany me to Worcester, to be lawfully questioned on a charge of murder. Open in the name of the Crown!'

Nothing happened. I looked about, scanning the windows on the upper floors, but saw no movement.

'Open!' Lisle repeated. 'Or I will force an entry.'

Again, silence - then came a sound, at which every man stirred. But it was not at the main door: instead, all eyes turned to see a shambling figure appear from a side entrance to the house: Matthew, Cobbett's old servant. He took a few paces forward, saw me and halted.

'Master Justice... thanks be to God.'

His voice shook, whether from fear or some other cause, I did not know. As the party watched, he sagged as if ready to drop, then made an effort to walk towards me. I dismounted quickly.

'Matthew? What on earth has happened...' I began – then

149

stopped as he broke into tears.

'God save you, sir...' Head bowed, he wiped his nose with a sleeve, and only then appeared to be aware of Lisle and the other men. Whereupon he lifted his hands in a gesture of helplessness, and let them fall.

'All is lost,' he cried. 'Ebbfield is lost - there is no-one left!'

* **

It took some time to calm the old servant, seated on a bench at the side of the courtyard. Sergeant Lisle and I, along with the constables and my people, gathered about him. Someone offered him a costrel of ale, from which he drank a little. Finally, with much sighing, he told his tale.

The servants, it seemed, had fled, deserting their master in a body. It had happened the previous afternoon, after a message arrived for Cobbett. Until then the place had been a hive of unrest, before word came that Jane and Alison were safe. Thereafter, it appeared that the master of Ebbfield had become somewhat irrational, threatening everybody in sight. He had even thrown open a chest of coins and scattered them about, calling his servants thieves and varlets, telling them to take their share and run like the rats they were. In the end he had shut himself away in his chamber, with only Eliza Dowling to attend him.

'Then where is he now?' Lisle demanded sternly. 'Do you tell me that he too has fled?'

'Nay...' Matthew peered up at him with rheumy eyes. 'I did not say so. But he gave orders not to be disturbed.'

The sergeant sniffed. 'Then I'm about to disappoint him.'

'See now... you don't understand,' the old man answered, in an agitated voice. 'He is not himself... he took to the chapel, early this morning. I fear for his safety...'

'How so?' I asked, throwing a swift glance at the sergeant. 'Is he alone, or...'

'I cannot be sure, sir,' came the mumbled reply.

'You say there are no servants remaining?' Lisle asked after a moment. 'Then, who made that barricade?'

'Dan Tait built it,' Matthew said, lowering his gaze. 'That rogue... he's been here again, demanding more money.'

'More money for what?' I enquired.

He looked up, letting out another sigh. 'I cannot tell you, Master Justice. There are terrible secrets here…' he glanced round. 'You come as rescuers, sirs, but too late. Mayhap it was ordained that the Cobbett line would fail, after more than a century. For myself…' he paused, then: 'This is not the family I served from boyhood. Hence, I will testify, as I should have done long ago. But I pray you, spare me further questions now.'

And with that he sat back and closed his eyes, seemingly without a care as to what followed.

I turned to Lisle. 'You hold the warrant, sergeant. Whatever action you take, we will aid you.'

'I know that, Master Justice.'

He drew himself to full height and looked round. 'We'll go to the chapel at once and arrest Cobbett - and if anyone tries to prevent us, they too will be taken. Given the man's likely state of mind, I ask you to charge your pistols.' He eyed the constables who nodded, content with his leadership.

'What of the nurse - Dowling?' I asked. 'She is still here, it seems.'

'I have no orders concerning her,' Lisle answered. 'Perhaps you should speak with her about the daughters, since you appear to be acting as their guardian.'

I made no reply; I knew Eliza Dowling was the last person Jane and Alison Cobbett wished to see. With a last glance at Matthew, slumped on the bench, I turned to the matter in hand.

The seven of us, armed and watchful, walked around the side of the house, to where the chapel stood. There was nobody in sight, nor was there a sound from the stables. Had even the horses bolted? Taut as a bowstring, I followed Lisle and his people up the pathway, with Elkins and Lockyer close behind. On reaching the door the sergeant lifted the latch and pushed, then turned to the rest of us.

'Locked.' He frowned. 'I'm loth to break it, this being a holy place.'

'Is there no other entrance?' One of the constables asked, a stocky fellow who looked as if he was spoiling for a fight. He busied himself making his pistol ready, as did the others.

'I think not,' I told him. My eyes strayed to the grassy patch where Hester and I had witnessed the burial of Susanna Cobbett, and found myself frowning: the grave was unmarked.

'Mayhap the old servant has a key,' Elkins said.

But Lisle turned away, and startled everyone by banging hard upon the door. 'Open up! He shouted, leaning close to the timbers. 'In the name of the Crown!'

We waited, every man alert. After a moment I believed I heard a voice, and saw that others had heard it too. But no-one came to the door. With the first sign of frustration he had shown, the sergeant rattled the latch and thumped again.

'It's no sin to break it,' the stocky constable remarked. 'We're on Crown business... a door can be repaired.'

I found myself glancing up at the stained-glass windows. I even wondered if some sense of remorse had come over Cobbett, in his predicament. Surely, with his daughters now free, he had guessed that all had been revealed? The thought raised my anger once again.

'I'm with the constable,' I said. 'If you wish to break the door in, my servants will assist.'

There was a pause, each man looking at his fellow. At last Lisle nodded, and would have given the order – whereupon there came a sound that made us start: the crash of breaking glass.

Whirling about, I saw a figure emerging clumsily from a broken window at the side of the chapel, cursing roundly. Coloured glass was everywhere, shards falling from his clothing as he squeezed himself through to land in an untidy heap. At once he scrambled to his feet - but on doing so, he found himself surrounded by a group of armed men. With a whimper, he stared about like a frightened rabbit.

'Tait?' I peered at him. 'What in God's name...'

'By the Christ, it's you!'

Dan Tait, sweating, hatless and dishevelled, returned my gaze. 'Are you come at me again? Why do you-' He broke off, his eyes on a pistol being levelled at his head. As the constables closed in, his face fell.

'Oh, Jesus... have mercy, masters,' he moaned. Wincing

suddenly, he looked down at his arm: his sleeve was torn, and blood ran freely. 'Now what have I done...'

'You've got yourself arrested, that's what.' Lisle was eying the man. 'I call it resisting officers in their legal duty. Or perhaps, aiding a felon...'

'I never!' Tait cried. 'I'm but a waterman – the Justice will tell you!' In a forlorn appeal for aid, he indicated me.

'Yet you built that foolish barricade, on the bridge,' Lisle retorted. 'Why?'

'Because he told me to!' Came the reply. 'The way he was, how could I refuse? He drew a fucking sword on me – like you did!' He glared at me, breathing hard, while blood continued to run down his arm and drip on to the path.

'So - you serve Giles Cobbett still,' I said. 'I wonder what else he's told you to do?'

He made no reply, but shook his head stubbornly.

'He's inside, then, your master?' Lisle jerked his thumb towards the door. 'Is he alone?'

For a moment the rogue looked as if he would refuse to answer again, but at last he shook his head. 'She's with him,' he muttered in a sour tone. 'Dowling... she always is.' His brow creased as he clutched his blood-soaked sleeve. 'See now, will you not fashion me a bandage? I could bleed to death!'

'That'd be no great loss,' one of the constables murmured, but received a disapproving look from the sergeant.

'In good time,' he said to Tait. 'Just now, I want some answers. What were you doing in the chapel, for one?'

'She begged me to go,' Tait said, glaring at him. 'She's afeared he'll do something rash, she said...' On a sudden, he let out a bitter laugh. 'I told her it was somewhat late to care about that, given all else he's done...'

'What do you mean?' Lisle broke in. 'That she fears Cobbett might take his own life?'

'By the Christ, I wish he would!' Tait threw back, his pain making him reckless. 'I wish he'd done it long ago, and saved us all from looking over our shoulders...' He turned a baleful eye on me. 'Belstrang knows what I mean,' he growled. 'How Cobbett pays others to take the risks, dirtying their hands and

153

their very souls, so he can keep himself free of blame!'

There was a short silence, with all eyes upon him: a sorry figure, when all was said and done. A boatman who could never make it pay, and had long ago turned his hand to other things, legal or otherwise. I thought of Berritt, who had wound up being dragged from the river by this man... and then, with a shock that chilled me from head to foot, I saw something else. I must have started, for every head was turned towards me.

'Howell Rhys,' I said, my hand going absently to my sword-hilt. 'By heaven... it was you killed him.'

There was an intake of breath all round. Lisle frowned at me, while Elkins gasped.

But it was true.

I knew it, even as I saw Tait grow pale, shaking his head loosely... until with a sigh he dropped to one knee, nursing his wound.

'She begged me to do that, too,' he said at last, his resistance drained. 'Dowling... she knew her master desired it. The boy could have accused him, so she badgered me, and-'

'And paid you too,' I finished. To which the ferryman looked down, and was silent.

I turned away from him. Now I could tell David ap Rhys who had murdered his son. But just then, it brought no relief.

TWENTY-THREE

It was all but over; the last throw of a misshapen dice in a desperate game. I sensed it then, as did the other men, as we prepared to force our way into the chapel.

Tait was gone, taken away with hands bound by one of the constables, to be conveyed to Worcester. There had been little need to question him further, for he had at last told the truth. He had been hired by Eliza Dowling, to remove an inconvenient witness for her master's sake. She had even provided him with poison to force down Howell Rhys's throat, after he had abducted the boy by night, beaten him and taken him to the Witching Pool.

With contempt, but with my anger dulled, I watched him disappear from sight, then joined the party at the chapel entrance. A crowbar had been found, and the stocky constable was forcing it between the doors. As the man put his weight to it, Lisle turned to me.

'I'll ask you to stay in the rear, Master Justice. I've no wish to see swords drawn.'

I gave a nod, my heart thudding a little; to be this close to seeing Cobbett brought to book for his crimes was exhilarating, and yet I was wary. I had no notion what to expect once we were inside... and soon, alarm rose anew. For as the lock began to break from the timbers, with much creaking and splintering, there came a sound from within: a woman's scream, shrill and piercing.

'It's Dowling.'

I glanced at the sergeant, saw his mouth tighten. He urged the constable to push harder until, after some grunting and straining, the man succeeded. The door flew inwards on a sudden, sending him off balance. As he fell forward, the others pushed past him. I followed with my own servants... to stop in my tracks.

Only a few yards from us, Eliza Dowling lay sprawled on the tiled floor in the aisle of the chapel. Her face was pale as chalk,

155

her gown soaked with blood. Seemingly in a daze, she looked up as the men bore down upon her.

'You are too late,' she said, her voice faint.

She lifted a hand feebly, placed it on the end of the nearest pew and tried to raise herself. But it was impossible; with a release of breath, she sank down again. Blood pooled upon the tiles, spreading outwards. Vaguely she looked down, as if unsure that it was hers. A trail of it led behind, showing how she had crawled towards the doors.

'I implored him to do it,' she said at last. 'There was no other way… the temple shall fall about Samson's ears, by his own volition.'

I looked beyond her, to the far end of the chapel. Others did the same, with muttered exclamations. Before the altar with his back to us, a figure was kneeling with head bowed, clad in only a shirt and breeches: Giles Cobbett, apparently indifferent to our presence. Candles burned upon the altar and in niches, giving the scene every appearance of calm and tranquillity – even of a kind of holiness.

'Will one of you stay with her?'

Lisle's voice brought us to order, as he gestured towards Eliza Dowling. One more glance at the woman was enough to convince me that she was close to death.

'Shall I fetch the old servant, sir?' Elkins spoke up. 'He might offer some comfort.'

I looked at Lisle, who nodded, whereupon Elkins went out at once. The rest of us – the sergeant and myself, my servant Lockyer and two constables – regarded the kneeling figure of the master of Ebbfield warily. With a last look at the dying woman, the sergeant stepped past her and started along the aisle… whereupon there was a sudden movement. Cobbett looked round, then got to his feet.

'Ah, nemesis!' He cried, his voice resounding off the walls. 'Welcome, one and all.'

There was a moment, then Lisle went forward with a hand on his sword. The others held back, but I could not. Walking up behind the sergeant, I halted beside him to face Cobbett… and was greeted with a bleak smile.

'Naturally you're here, Belstrang,' he said. 'You wouldn't have missed it, would you? You and your sword of justice…' his gaze flickered to my rapier in its scabbard. 'And now you have satisfaction…'

He broke off, as if surprised to see pistols pointing in his direction. He himself was unarmed, his shirt creased and sweat-stained, his hair untidy; he looked as if he had not slept in days. The difference between this cornered wolf, and the man I had last seen in hunting attire mounted on a fine horse, was stark. I drew breath, and was somewhat relieved when Lisle's voice broke the silence.

'Giles Cobbett, I arrest you for the murder of your daughter Susanna Cobbett and her unborn child,' he announced, keeping his voice clear of emotion. 'You are to accompany me to Worcester, there to await trial at the Midsummer Assizes.'

Another silence fell, as the echo of his words died away. Cobbett allowed his eyes to range over the men who had come to take him. He remained calm… too calm, I thought, and on a sudden I found myself speaking.

'There's also the murder of your servant, Dowling,' I said, with a sideways look at Lisle. 'Even if she claims she begged you to do it.'

'Well, so she did.' Cobbett nodded. 'She was destined to die an old maid, childless and miserable. It was an act of mercy-'

'That's enough speech-making, sir.' His voice cold as steel, the sergeant took a step nearer to the man. 'You must put yourself in my charge, and let us convey you from here.'

He turned briefly to his men, who moved to obey, but at once a warning rang in my head – and even as I cried out, I was aware of a rapid movement from Cobbett. Whirling round, he knocked candles aside, spilling molten wax on to the altar cloth. At once flames sprang up, causing Lisle to lurch forward. But as he did so, Cobbett darted to the side of the altar – and in a moment, a sword appeared in his hand. It was shiny with blood: the blood of Eliza Dowling.

'Well now…' breathing fast, his eyes wild with a kind of delight, the master of Ebbfield faced his would-be captors. 'Let's see you take me into your charge now, shall we?'

Following that, everything happened with speed: a tableau lit by the eerie glow of flames and guttering candles. There was the deafening roar of a pistol-shot, which missed its mark as Cobbett skipped aside. Lifting his rapier, he lunged, stabbing at the air. Then, seeing the sergeant's hand fly to his sword-hilt, he jabbed... and a muffled cry came from Lisle's mouth. The blade had pierced his side, causing blood to well...

'Get back, sir!'

Lockyer was at my side, shoving me away. Taking hold of Lisle, who was swaying on his feet, he thrust him aside too, one eye on the crazed figure of the sword-wielding assailant. But even as he squared up to the man, there came another explosion from close by, as the other constable fired.

Half-deafened by the pistol's roar, I watched as gore splattered from the forehead of Giles Cobbett. His sword landed on the floor with a clang; his arm dropped, his body loose and lifeless as he fell on his back and lay still.

It was over.

But the altar burned fiercely, charred scraps of broidered cloth falling about the dead man. Already the wooden panelling was catching fire. Somewhat dazed, I saw figures hurry past me. Then Lockyer was bustling me out, one constable was helping Lisle towards the door while the other went forward to seize Cobbett's feet by the bootheels. As smoke began to fill the chapel, he dragged the man along the blood-stained floor, coughing and wheezing. Whereupon, coming to my senses at last, I found myself looking down at another corpse: that of Eliza Dowling, now slumped beside a pew with her eyes open, staring at nothing.

'Bring her out,' I ordered. And when Lockyer hesitated, I pointed. 'Go on – I'm unhurt.'

He turned to obey, while I got myself to the doors which were wide open, letting in a breeze to fan the flames. Once outside, breathing fast, I found Lisle sitting on the ground, pressing a bloody hand to his side. Meeting my gaze, he managed a nod.

'It's but a shallow wound... I'll staunch the flow.'

I was about to go to him when I heard running feet, and turned to see Elkins hurrying up with Matthew behind him. Seeing flames licking at the edges of the broken chapel window, the old man stopped in horror.

'God help us,' he cried, his face haggard. 'Where's the master?'

Nobody answered. Two bodies were being carried from the doomed building: those of Cobbett and his devoted servant, the woman who had hoped in vain to become his wife. The constables laid them together on the grassy patch, close to the grave of Susanna. Meanwhile my servants came to attend me, relieved that I had taken no harm. I mumbled words of reassurance, whereupon quite quickly a weariness came upon me: one of sheer relief.

'He's paid for his crimes,' I said, drawing deep breaths. 'Not in the way I hoped, but…'

I trailed off, allowing myself a last look at the man who had done such terrible deeds; even now, it chills me to think on the evil that went on in his house – and at last, in his chapel. That too was now destroyed: there was a well near the stables, but it was too late to save the building. Within a half-hour, by which time some order had been established, the arresting party could only watch as flames leaped through the roof, shooting skywards as the wind took them.

When we made our way back to the courtyard to arrange our departure, only Matthew remained with head bowed, weeping silently at the chapel's destruction, and the end of the once-noble house of Cobbett.

Since the man left no sons, his name would die with it.

* * *

It was a sombre group which eventually made its way out of the courtyard and rumbled over the bridge, to take the road to Worcester. A cart had been found, and two ageing horses to draw it: the last ones left in the Ebbfield stables. Cobbett's fine hunting horse was gone, likely stolen by one of his grooms. In the cart were the covered bodies of Cobbett and Eliza Dowling. Lisle, against advice, insisted on riding, his body bound tightly with cloths taken from the house. In fact, once some of the men ventured inside, they had found the place stripped of almost everything of value, from plate and hangings to candlesticks.

The manor had a forlorn air, as if life had departed - which in truth, it had.

I rode behind the cart with Elkins and Lockyer. We had said little since watching the chapel burn, but I now took occasion to praise them for their actions. Without their aid, I realised, matters might have taken an even darker turn.

'Cobbett meant to die, sir,' Lockyer said, after a while. 'I've seen men make their last stand, when they know there's no other way out.'

'Yet, it was a coward's way,' Elkins muttered, with a shake of his head. 'He couldn't face up to what he'd done, so chose to cheat justice as he's cheated the hangman.'

I said nothing: on a sudden, I thought of Boyd and his views on self-murder. Did Cobbett's final acts amount to such, I wondered - suicide by the action of constables? Doubtless it would serve for a topic of debate, one day.

'What do you mean to do with him, sir?'

Lockyer nodded towards Matthew, who was sitting in the cart with the bodies: a shrivelled figure, his arms wrapped about him.

'I mean to offer him a place in my service,' I replied. 'He's honest and loyal, even if his master was unworthy of him.' I found a wry smile forming. 'Though heaven knows what Childers will say.'

The other two exchanged looks, but made no reply.

And by the afternoon we were riding through my gates, all duties discharged, content to let the peace of Thirldon envelop us one again.

TWENTY-FOUR

May was over, and June came in with clear skies. King James, we heard, was still riding about Scotland, destined to end his sojourn in Glasgow and then return south by way of Carlisle. Childers wondered if he would pass through Worcester, which turned out not to be the case. But see now, I digress.

There was much to be done in the days following the death of Giles Cobbett. I spent time in my chamber, penning a report of what had occurred along with letters to various parties, Boyd among them. I was uncertain as to what would happen now that Cobbett was gone; but in the end, matters seemed to arrange themselves.

The first news to bring comfort was that the charge of murder against Agnes Mason was to be withdrawn. The surprise was that the tidings came to me from Standish himself, brought to Thirldon by his clerk.

'The Justice is most troubled by these events, Master Belstrang,' the man said stiffly, as we stood in the courtyard that morning. 'He intends to conduct further investigations, but I can tell you that the ferryman and the farmer, Humphreys, have been put to question and have confirmed your testimony. They will face trial soon, the likely outcome of which you may anticipate.'

He paused, noting my evident relief, then continued: 'The Justice also wishes me to convey his heartfelt thanks for your diligent efforts in uncovering these matters...'

'When will Mason be released?' I broke in. 'And what arrangements will be made to convey her out of the city?'

The clerk frowned. 'I have no knowledge of that, sir. My understanding is that she is yet confined at the Guildhall.' Having said what he came to say, he proffered a sealed letter, which I accepted. But as he remounted his horse, I stayed him.

'Pray tell the Justice that I'm grateful for his courtesy,' I said. 'I'll write to him soon, with a small request that I'm certain he will be willing to grant.'

If he was surprised by my apparent confidence, the man gave no sign. He signalled assent, whereupon I watched him ride out of the gates just as Childers emerged from the house.

'Mistress Jane and Mistress Alison wish to speak with you,' he said. I turned to him, wondering why he appeared so cheerful this morning.

'It seems their preparations are almost complete,' he added. 'Their mother's sister awaits them at Gloucester, where they will be made welcome.'

'I know that already,' I said, eying him suspiciously.

It was common knowledge at Thirldon that the sisters had been in correspondence with their aunt. While grateful for the shelter they had enjoyed under my protection, they were ready to depart. The tragic events at Ebbfield had affected them deeply, but in the end their emotions were tempered with relief. A nightmare was ended, Jane had said; her hopes were for a new beginning.

I went indoors and sent word to both girls to come to my parlour. They arrived soon after with Hester, and after a few pleasantries I broached the matter of their leaving.

'With your approval, it will be tomorrow, Master Justice,' Jane said.

'Have you informed your aunt?' I enquired, taken aback.

'I have,' she replied, somewhat quickly.

'I told them it would be acceptable,' Hester said, her eyes upon mine. 'It's but a matter of someone driving the coach.'

'The coach?' I echoed. 'It hasn't been used in years... it would have to be repaired.'

'I've asked the men to look it over,' Hester said. And when I began to look displeased: 'You've had so much to do of late, we thought it best not to trouble you. Elkins will drive the coach to Gloucester, if you can spare him from his duties. Surely you would not expect daughters of good breeding to travel by the same manner in which they arrived here – I mean in a plain farm-cart?'

In some consternation I looked to Jane and Alison, who sat silent and erect. Their meekness, however, appeared a show: I even suspected here was a hint of a smile beneath Jane's expression. In truth, I thought, my authority nowadays was become a shadow of what it had been. I was about to form some reply, when Alison spoke.

'We have a request to make of you, sir,' she said. 'That our servant Matthew be permitted to come with us.'

So that was it. 'Is he not content here?' I asked. 'I understood he...'

I stopped myself: now I saw why Childers was in such good humour. It was no secret that he disliked having Matthew about the house: a forlorn figure who had aged even further since the violent demise of his old life, and who forgot an order within minutes of it being given.

'Very well...' I let out a sigh, which seemed to bring general relief. 'Indeed, I would never prevent him... he is of your household, after all.'

'He was, sir,' Jane said. 'There is no household now. But Matthew has been faithful all our lives... it is only fitting that he be allowed to spend what time he has left with us.'

I gave a nod; on a sudden, there seemed little more to be said. The burials, which I had helped arrange, were over, the sisters' wish to be spared attendance being honoured. As for Cobbett's property, that was another matter; I envisaged suits, claims and counter-claims from relatives and creditors which would keep the lawyers busy for years. Thankfully that was not the concern of a former magistrate, who was anticipating a quiet summer of cards and fishing.

And so we parted, the sisters expressing thanks before returning to their arrangements. A maid had been ordered to help them with the packing. Shortly after Cobbett's death, I had sent men to Ebbfield to recover the sisters' possessions from their chambers, though it seemed there was little left to be retrieved. But no matter, Jane said: their old life was gone, and should be put behind them.

On the morrow, Hester and I bade them farewell.

It was a sad occasion, because we had come to see them not merely as guests of Thirldon, but as friends. They were close to tears as they got into the old coach, barely used since my father's time but seemingly serviceable. Matthew held the door open, before closing it and climbing up onto the driver's seat with difficulty, to seat himself beside Elkins. My groom was content, being in possession of a sum for expenses: the journey would take a whole day, which would entail his spending the night at Gloucester. As he shook the reins and urged the horses forward, Jane and Alison waved from the open windows. Then they were gone: the last of their family to dwell in this shire, perhaps for ever.

But there was a matter of importance yet remaining, which I approached with a mixture of feelings. The opportunity came two days later, when I received the letter I had hoped for from Standish. By the evening I was in Worcester, making my way up the steps of the Guildhall, where to my surprise I was soon facing Sergeant Lisle once again. I had not seen him since the debacle at Ebbfield, but was pleased to find him restored to his stolid self.

'The wound is healing, Master Justice,' he said. 'Though I'm a mite sore in the mornings.' He regarded me with his shrewd look. 'You are in health, I trust?'

I assured him I was, and spoke briefly of recent events: the departure of the Cobbett girls along with their servant. Yet he seemed unwilling to dwell on the matter. I believed I knew why, but it was only later, with the passage of time, that I gained a truer understanding: that Lisle saw the grim climax of events at Ebbfield as a failure on his part. To a man like him, duty was everything. His orders had been to arrest Giles Cobbett and bring him in to await trial, and he had fallen short.

'Worcester is abuzz with the affair,' he told me, with a wry look. 'Cobbett will achieve a fame he never expected, if not for reasons he'd have wished.' He gestured towards the stairhead. 'Well now, shall we proceed?'

So, for the last time I followed him down to the gloomy cellars, but as we reached the lower floor I stayed him. 'I heard she is in better spirits, is it so?'

'Indeed, sir... her health is fair, given the weeks she's spent here. And I'd wager today will bring the healing she needs.' He paused, then: 'The matter has been arranged as you requested, by permission of the Justice. Are you prepared?'

'Most certainly,' I answered - which was a lie. I was aflutter with doubt, at pains to keep it hidden. And as we walked to the end of the cellar, my unease arose as to whether I had done aright.

I would bring Agnes Mason away, out of Worcester with speed before the gates shut for the night. It was believed to be the best course of action, given feelings that still prevailed towards the supposed witch. The knowledge of Giles Cobbett's deeds that had leaked out was piecemeal, and doubtless clouded with gossip and rumour. And though there was no crowd of angry townsfolk outside the Guildhall now, the need for caution was paramount.

Yet, I would not be alone to escort Agnes to freedom: my companion-in-arms, as I had requested as a favour from Standish, was now standing before me by the door of her cell: her jailer, grim-faced and silent.

'Now, Master Burton,' I said, with forced cheerfulness. 'Are you ready for our little journey?'

He barely grunted, but under Lisle's eye was forced to do his office. Wordlessly, he took the bundle of keys from his belt and fitted one to the lock. As the door swung open he stood back, his eyes on the floor.

'Mistress Mason?' I took a step inside, peering about in the gloom; it seemed an age since I was last here. I was rewarded with a rustling of straw - and at once, she was before me.

'Master Justice.'

She met my gaze, causing me to draw a sharp breath. I'm uncertain what I had expected to find: a figure emaciated and shrunken, perhaps, hair matted with neglect – but I was wrong. She appeared unchanged, standing calm and erect in a different frock to the one I remembered... whereupon she guessed my thoughts, and reminded me.

'It's the one you sent,' she murmured; she even managed a faint smile. 'Whoever wore it must have been close to me in size. It's somewhat grand, yet I'm most beholden to her – and to you.'

'Are you ready to go?' I asked, somewhat briskly. 'I have horses...'

She gave a shrug. 'I have nothing to take with me, save the lice.'

I turned and got myself outside, so abruptly that Burton took an involuntary step back. As Agnes too left the cell he stiffened, scowling at his boots. But nothing was said as the four of us, led by Lisle, walked to the stairs and began to climb. Up in the hall people stared at the ex-prisoner, some in unfriendly fashion; not everyone was pleased to see the one they called Mother Blackcat walk free.

But we passed to the doors without challenge, to emerge in the gathering dusk. Here atop the steps, the sergeant-at-arms and I said our brief farewell. As he went back inside he threw me a warm look, that spoke of both friendship and respect.

Standing close to Agnes, I realised that this was her first moment outdoors in more than a month. I turned to see her with eyes closed, breathing deeply in the eventide air. 'It's but a short while now,' I said. 'Once we're clear of the city, you will be with your family within the hour.'

I turned to Burton, who stood like a post, his lips tight-shut. He was armed with pistol and poniard, and wore a coat that, I now realised, had a hood.

'Are you afraid someone will recognise you?' I said, keeping my face blank.

'No more than you are – sir,' he answered. 'But I'm under orders to be guided by you... can we go?'

I pointed to where the boy I had hired stood with the horses: Leucippus, a mare for Agnes and a horse from the Guildhall stable, saddled and ready. So, with a glance from side to side, we stepped down to the street and walked quickly to the mounts. I had to help Agnes, who was unused to riding. But once in the saddle, she took the rein and threw me a look of relief.

'I had begun to think this day would never come,' she said.

I made no reply, but tugged Leucippus's rein and led the way through the streets. Agnes rode with difficulty, trying to stay close while Burton brought up the rear, hooded and watchful. But the town was quiet, and nothing prevented us. Within minutes, as church bells clanged, we had made our way to the west gate, then passed through to the bridge. There was a creak as the great doors closed behind us, then we were out on the road, gathering pace. In relief, I relaxed in the saddle and allowed Agnes to draw alongside me.

'I have not yet thanked you,' she said.

'Your freedom is thanks enough,' I said, and promptly cursed myself for my feebleness.

'It is not,' she replied. But after that, she was silent.

The journey downriver to Powick was an easy enough ride in the dusk, with a rising moon which would help to light my way homewards. My fears of being waylaid proved groundless, which occasioned some relief from Burton. As we neared the Teme bridge, having kept in the rear for most of the way, he urged his horse forward and gained my attention.

'This is as far as I go,' he said. 'The village will be taking to their beds, and the road ahead is clear.'

I drew rein, as did Agnes, who eyed the man warily. A moment passed, but he could not depart so easily. He had his orders, and under my gaze strove to execute them with what grace he could muster.

'I ask your pardon, Mistress, for what I did back at the Guildhall,' he muttered, avoiding her eye. And when she made no response: 'I have something for you.'

He fumbled at his belt and produced a small purse. Its contents, of course, had been provided by me, but I had no wish for Agnes to know it. She hesitated, then took the purse in silence. Whereupon the man wheeled his mount, shook the rein and rode away without looking back. Even from a distance, I saw his shoulders sag in relief.

As he disappeared, Agnes turned in the saddle to face me. 'This is your doing,' she said.

I shook my head. Her eyes shone in the dim light, or so it seemed; what an old fool I had become.

'Let's get clear of Powick,' I said. 'Then we should walk the horses, for I have things to tell you.'

We passed through the village, where all was quiet save for noises from the inn. Once on the lane to Cobbett's tenant farms, we slowed pace and at last dismounted. As I helped her down from the mare she stumbled, allowing the weight of her body to fall against mine; and though she righted herself at once, it was a taut moment. Had she given me the chance I would have embraced her... but it was not to be.

'What is it you wished to say?' she asked.

I drew a breath and told what had happened at Ebbfield, of which she had heard nothing; she knew that the charges against her were annulled, but not why. Hence, as we began leading the horses onwards, I found myself giving her the whole tale in brief, including the arrest of Tait and Humphreys. And when we drew close to the turning to his farm, she halted.

'I will go to his wife soon,' she said. 'There may be things she and I should speak of.'

We moved on without further word. Night was falling fast, and I was keen to deliver her safely to her home, where Edward Mason and his wife would be waiting; a letter had been sent, with the news they craved. Yet at the same time I wished the last part of the journey would pass slowly, so that I might have these moments with her. After a while I ventured to ask what she would do now: would the family wish to remain, as tenants of whoever took over Ebbfield?

'I cannot say,' she answered. 'Perhaps we'll go elsewhere, if we can.'

On a sudden I halted, realising where we were. To our right, barely visible in the gloom, was the path to the Witching Pool. Agnes stopped walking too.

'I doubt if anyone will go there for a good while,' she said, nodding towards the treeline. 'It's a place of death, and old beliefs will linger long after I'm gone. Yet in time, people may forget...' she touched my arm, causing me to turn sharply. 'As must you, Master Justice.'

'I cannot,' I said.

Yet, here it was: what was always going to be our last moment together. As I looked down, she lifted her face and kissed me hard on the mouth, then drew away.

'I will walk by myself from here,' she said. 'I like to walk in the night... and when I greet Edward and Isabel, it's best we are alone.'

She had let the mare's rein fall and was already backing along the narrow path, then she stopped.

'I know why Giles Cobbett wanted me dead,' she said. 'He was afraid of me – afraid I would divine what he did to his daughter, as he believed I could divine for buried gold.'

I gazed at her. 'And yet, you are no cunning-woman… or so you told me.'

'I did,' she answered. 'But I see your fortune, Master Justice.' She managed a smile, then: 'I say you have little to fear, and everything to hope for. But wherever you are, whatever you do, you are always here.'

She put her hand to her heart, and pressed it there. Then she turned about and walked away with a sure and steady step, to vanish into the gloom.

**

I took my time riding homewards, leading the mare – Hester's mare, in fact. All the while, I thought on the last hour I had spent with the woman accused of witchcraft; one who, I now believe, had always known more than she let anyone see. And though parting from her was a cup of bitterness, it had to be swallowed. I knew it as I walked Leucippus back towards Powick, leaving Newland Wood and its dark pool behind. I had no wish to go there again; besides, the fishing was too poor even to countenance.

On a sudden, I thought of riding to see Boyd on the morrow and suggesting a trip upriver, which lifted my spirits somewhat. First, of course, I would buy him a dinner at The Old Talbot and talk things over as we had always done, before events intervened.

But the storm had passed. Breathing in the balmy night air, I saw the rooftops of Powick village ahead and urged the horses to a better pace… and at the last, I found myself thinking on the legend of Offa's gold.

It has never been found; I wonder if it ever will?

Printed in Great Britain
by Amazon